THE ROAD BEYOND
THE BOLTED DOOR

THE ROAD BEYOND
THE BOLTED DOOR

Corine Channell

gatekeeper press™

Columbus, Ohio

The Road Beyond The Bolted Door

Published by Gatekeeper Press
2167 Stringtown Rd, Suite 109
Columbus, OH 43123-2989
www.GatekeeperPress.com

ISBN (paperback): 9781662926013

DEDICATION

When I first began putting this book together, I knew exactly WHO I wanted to dedicate it to - my beautiful, strong daughter Katrina Joy.

Pretty cool when you raise your own best friend.

She has been my steady on, and my constant. Because without her being willing and able to take this journey WITH me, I am not sure I would have been able to allow the painful healing to run its course.

Her favorite poem is *"Footprints In The Sand"*, a beautiful poem written by Mary Stevenson, in 1939. It is a prayer that speaks of how God is ALWAYS with us, even when we think we are alone - and if we turn around and look back on the sands of time, many times we can only see His footprints. We don't see OUR footprints, because HE was carrying us.

On MY road less traveled, Jesus and Katrina walked with me, and at some points both carried me or dragged me. NOW I can look back, and see ALL three sets of our footprints in the sand - walking together. *"If you want to go fast, go alone. If you want to go far, go together."* (African Proverb)

TABLE OF CONTENTS

FOREWORD

I was going to write a review of *The Road Beyond The Bolted Door* as just a pre reader, but the more I read the more I realized I needed to write the foreword, as Corine's daughter. The thing is, I never knew she was so broken; she was just mom!

I've walked beside her over the last few years on her journey to facing her past. We've cried so many tears, sometimes I didn't think we could go on anymore. Every year that passes I see her stand a little taller and speak a little louder. I've watched my quiet, meek mannered mother become a warrior fighting to break free from her past, so she can help other people to break free from theirs.

She talks about wanting a do-over or feeling like she showed up late to a party. She wasn't late; God still used her as she was. In spite of her brokenness she was still able to give her 6 kids wonderful childhood memories. (As well as many other kids along the way that she didn't give birth to.) The MANY birthday parties, prize bags for every occasion, Friday night pizza, camping trips etc. made her such a special mom. She loved us no matter what, and when I look back I don't see the brokenness, I just see my mom.

If you have any sort of abuse in your life you need to read this book; it will give you hope for your own future! You're not too damaged for God to heal you.

Katrina Clement/Daughter of the Author Corine Channell

Corine takes us on a healing journey in her book, *The Road Beyond the Bolted Door.* This journey is an affirmation for the soul of one who has been victimized. It leaves the reader feeling affirmed, enlightened, and armed with knowledge. As you walk this journey with Corine, she will be completely honest with you; the road to healing is a process, a process that will at times be painful. *"Breaking free is scary business! It takes more strength than you never knew you could muster up, and it has to start with resolve to NEVER retreat."* (Chapter 3 - "Rising From The Depths") But don't worry, she holds your hand through every page, she calms you with poetry and song lyrics from others who have walked the journey before you and she keeps you laughing with her humor and wit. But most importantly, she points you to Jesus, the lover of our souls. For without Him none of us would have hope for the future.

~Milinda Mugford/Teacher

Corine's book *The Road Beyond the Bolted Door* helped me as a victim. I suffer from the lasting effects of sexual abuse. She mentions healing is a process. She is correct; healing takes time. After reading her book I don't feel alone. She has shown me strength and courage with her words, songs, and scriptures. I know I will be ok, and it is because of her. This book is a must for anyone suffering from any type of abuse.

~Carissa Cron/Survivor of sexual abuse

When I read the first book *Beyond The Bolted Door* I was immediately drawn by the quote from a song

- *"there's a part of me I can't get back, a little girl grew up too fast."* And so it was the beginning of my story as well, though not one of the sexual abuse, but I was orphaned at the age of 11. Case in point we all have our stories to tell, and we all have our own bolted doors to unlock. I applaud the author for this second book *The Road Beyond The Bolted Door*, for opening her heart, becoming transparent and vulnerable and risky, to share the hard and lonely road she's walked. I truly believe her heart's desire is to help others, to give them hope, and the keys to no longer be victims but victors. That we would discover all things work together for good and there is a restored purpose for our lives. Broken no more.

~Mary Roth/Retired

The Road Beyond The Bolted Door is such an amazing read. It is intense and deep, but it is such a helpful guide to help overcome your pain and help you heal! This book really helped me understand that I am not alone! Healing hurts, but this book definitely helped me navigate my way through the pain! Not only will it help your healing heart but it will let you know that what you're experiencing is normal; hurting is normal and we're not alone! The road beyond my own bolted door is now much easier after reading this book, and I really think it would be helpful to so many others! I would 100% recommend this book!

~Katie Cobb/Abuse survivor

As I found myself immersed deeply into the pages of *The Road Beyond The Bolted Door* it became quite apparent to me that Corine was no longer referring to **her** door anymore. Although; I believe that was her intention. THIS *masterpiece* is about everyone else's doors which have been bolted shut! Doors of oppression, lust, evil, depression, unhealthiness, financial ruin, war, abuse (whether mental, verbal, spiritual or physical), pain, loss, regrets, etc. "It's a proven fact that some homeless people, if given a house, would eventually go back to the street, because it felt safer." Metaphorically, that is one of the most powerfully accurate sentences Corine wrote. Not only is it true of a lot of homeless, but it's also very true of a lot of former prisoners. Unfortunately many fall prey to this phenomenon over and over again, in any predicament whether perceived good or evil.

In the first book *Beyond The Bolted Door,* Corine used a derivative of the word **free** about 26 times. She was asking and seeking. While reading *The Road Beyond The Bolted Door* I noticed Corine used the words; free, freedom, freely (or some derivative of free) just about 50 times. Almost double! The Bible states in Matthew 7:7 - *"Ask, and it shall be given you; seek, and ye shall find; knock, and it shall be opened unto you."* That last part is referring to the opening of a door! In this book the door opens the freedom road not only for Corine, but for a multitude of others who will read it, myself included.

William Shakespeare wrote in *The Taming of the Shrew* {Act 3: Scene 2} - *"The door is open ... there lies your way."* If you or anyone you know have some bolted doors, get this masterpiece. *The Road Beyond The Bolted Door* is a must read.

~Joe Wooley/Actor/U.S. Marine (Ret.)

PREFACE

The pain from our healing is not sent to kill us - it is sent to make us stronger and able to sustain ourselves first and then others. *"To sustain means to give support to, to hold up, to bear, meeting our own needs without compromising the ability of future generations to meet their own needs."* (Wikipedia)

I think this quote from my favorite childhood stuffed animal Winnie the Pooh, sums up my simple WHY for this book -

> *"Then would you read a Sustaining Book, such as would help and comfort a Wedged Bear in Great Tightness?"*

("*Winnie the Pooh*" by AA Milne)

I am writing to sustain, help, and comfort any of you who feel wedged in great tightness.

INTRODUCTION

My first book *Beyond The Bolted Door* was me shattering the silence of my past history of sexual abuse and its harmful effects on the seasons of my life. I did NOT realize that the road I would need to walk to healing beyond my own bolted door would be unrecognizable to me. Our lives are governed by roads. Roads are pathways. They take us places. Simple concept, right? Except when we all of a sudden realize we are lost, and we have no idea which road is the right one. I was not prepared to heal from my shame and the burden of a secret carried for so long, and reappear as a stranger. I thought I would know WHO I was when I ran into myself again. I really, really expected this. And THIS is NOT what happened.

This second book *The Road Beyond The Bolted Door* is my NOW as I proceed on my journey to find innocence lost, wholeness and healing on my own road less traveled. To heal FROM the healing itself is a hard road to travel.

It is an interesting experience to not have any idea what the next chapter will even be about. I can't plan it. I write as it happens, as I experience it and as I learn it. This is the real deal. There have been a lot of unexpected and unanticipated consequences from healing - both in my personal life, in my emotions, in my head, in my heart, and in my soul. I feel the need to explore and share these many unexpected and unanticipated consequences for anyone who may need to know what to expect on their own road beyond the bolted door.

In sharing my journey of healing, my hope is that this book will be a road map or a survival guide for someone who feels alone and misunderstood, or even shunned and cast aside on their own healing journey. At the very least I want to arm you with eye opening knowledge and a clear understanding of all the layers of abuse, as being the destructive enemy that it is. And help you rediscover innocence, faith, and hope.

Yes, the truth sets us free but first, it hurts. *"Start by doing what's necessary; then do what's possible; and suddenly you are doing the impossible."* (Francis of Assisi)

CHAPTER ONE
The Road Less Traveled

~As you travel your own road less traveled, may all the shame and blame and pain RIP as you get your life back, little by little, step by step~

The narrative poem below, titled "The Road Not Taken" was written by Robert Frost in 1916, and I bet he never expected that we would be quoting it and gaining wisdom from its message more than a century later.

"Two roads diverged in a yellow wood,

*And sorry I could **not** travel both*

And be one traveler, long I stood

And looked down one as far as I could

To where it bent in the undergrowth;

Then took the other, as just as fair,

And having perhaps the better claim,

Because it was grassy and wanted wear;

Though as for that the passing there

Had worn them really about the same,

And both that morning equally lay

In leaves no step had trodden black.

Oh, I kept the first for another day!

Yet knowing how way leads on to way,

I doubted if I should ever come back.

I shall be telling this with a sigh

Somewhere ages and ages hence:

Two roads diverged in a wood, and I—

I took the one less traveled by,

And that has made all the difference."

For me, that last line hits the nail on the head about how I feel right now. I AM on the road less traveled. I chose it when I finally broke my silence over sexual abuse, and changed course.

There is a brief moment between before and after. Perhaps this is where we reflect, change, decide - trying to weigh out if we WANT to proceed into the after. There is always a cost to consider. *"For which of you, intending to build a tower, sitteth not down first, and counteth the cost, whether he have sufficient to finish it? Lest haply, after he hath laid the foundation, and is not able to finish it, all that behold it begin to mock him, Saying, This man began to build, and was not able to finish."* (Luke 14:28-30) The easy path is achieved without great effort and presents few difficulties. The hard path requires counting the cost, and needs much effort and/or skill to accomplish, understand and get through. These two roads are complete opposites.

Over the past few years I backtracked on treacherous paths into the cesspool (underground storage of sewage/filth) of my hidden past, dealing with its ugliness, shame and destructive effects on my life - I felt like I HAD to, if for no other reason than to break it from being a curse that would come down through the generations of those I love the most. I took a journey back to open the bolted door of my life, to expose the secret I had kept my entire life that had wreaked havoc in my life.

"There is no greater agony than bearing an untold story inside you." (Maya Angelou) Finally I became strong enough to tell my story. What utter relief. Mission accomplished. Book published. Fearless. Head held high. Marching into battle swinging my sword. Right? You'd think. Um, not so much like that at all.

Suddenly though, I had no more words. I had no smiles. I had no inspiration. I had no joy. I felt like an outsider looking in on my own life. So, what was THAT all about?! Hadn't I just embraced my healing, found my freedom - didn't I just win the fight of my life? The minute I released my book publicly, I privately went into full on panic mode and went and took a long nap. And from there, if someone told me they ordered my book, I took a nap. If someone told me they were reading my book, I took a nap. If someone sent me a message about my book, I took a nap. A nap was clearly a better escape mechanism than all the other options.

Finally I was like - what the what is wrong with me!?!?! Well, it WAS a long journey. I think when it was over, I was just - tired. In the words of Forrest Gump, *"I'm pretty tired. I think I'll go home now."* You can think better after you rest. So, I learned to rest my brain, my heart, and my body. Now I get it. And my naps have gotten to be few and far between.

It pains me to say that I need to warn you how painful heal-ing is. You have likely heard the expression *"Ignorance is bliss"*, which is a phrase that originated with Thomas Gray in his 1768 *"Ode on a Distant Prospect of Eton College"*. I NOW understand what that means. I understand WHY I never came forward or told my truth sooner. It was much easier to just ignore it and hope it went away. For me this looked like that phrase, *"hear no evil, see no evil, speak no evil."* I lived like that in SO many ways. I shelved my abuse and I moved on further and further away from it, yet - I dragged it with me like heavy chains attached to my soul. I just didn't really know that. It was weighing me down, crippling my walk through this life. I didn't know how heavy it was until I acknowledged it there. THEN it became almost unbearable. I kid you not nor will I lie - healing hurts! BUT it has to be done. I mean, TO heal you MUST heal.

When I had double knee replacement surgery, they beat my old knees into smithereens - which means, they smashed them into small broken pieces. They destroyed all the arthritis, all the decay, all the lameness, all the broken and fractured parts of both of my entire knees. I am SO glad I was NOT awake to witness that. (I have been told they use an actual hammer.)

One week later, I ran in a 5K with my new knees and I won, as I outran every other runner - all 246 of them. Kidding. Of course. I still have not run in a 5K. And safe to say I probably never will. Although, never say never!

Basically, I have learned that AFTER you heal from anything, you need therapy, which technically means you need treatment for relief and healing to a physical injury or mental disorder. Therapy is an active process. It builds muscle in the body OR in the soul, and is extremely important. And there is NO shame attached to requiring it to heal fully. I was in excruciating pain. I needed pain medicine. I needed ice packs. I needed a walker. I needed physical therapy. **I needed help**. It was a 'have to' in my healing because I had to relearn how to walk! Doing knee lifts and stretches to make metal knees bend is as painful as it sounds! It took a long time for my knees to heal; not gonna lie. But little by little, my new knees made me feel like I was bionic; reborn even - like I had my teen knees back! They bend and stretch; they don't hurt; they are still going when the rest of me that is NOT bionic has come to a standstill. And there finally came that amazing year when I could walk 2 miles a day with my granddaughter in her stroller. I knew. I KNEW my new knees were no longer broken and were now a brand new functioning part of me. I think walking it out is ultimately HOW my knees healed. I had to just keep walking. It has been a 10 year journey from the initial restructure of my knees until now. **Healing takes time.**

So, WHY would I think I could face my mental demons head on, slay them, and then just walk away like I had NOT just battled for my life? Hello. It is as painful as it sounds! My dear friend said something so profoundly simple to me as I tried to put my frustrated feelings into words to her - she gently said, *"You need recovery therapy."* I instantly felt those words. It was like a **light** came on in my soul! Recovery is a process of reclaiming possession or control of something lost or stolen! I knew right then I needed to reclaim my stolen innocence AND reconstruct my broken soul.

When you decide to get help for yourself, for whatever issue you have - whether physical or mental, it first comes with an admission that something is wrong - something is not up to par. Then comes that stage of denial - I know something is wrong, but do I really want to know what IT is. Do I really want to go through what will need to be done to get answers? *"It's not forgetting that heals. It's remembering."* (Amy Greene) THIS is so true.

We avoid truth because truth hurts. and it requires change. and it is out of our comfort zone. Is the pain of healing really worth knowing the truth, no matter how dark and deep and terrible? I mean, really - who says, bring on the pain! Healing is painful. Hear me. In fact, let me say it again - **healing is painful.** Anyone recovering from a surgery knows what I am talking about. Yes, you have new knees. Yes, your bone has been reset. Yes, you beat Covid. But there is an aftermath. And really, it is initially why we wait so long before we go see a doctor or get a diagnosis or start treatment. We KNOW it will change everything and we KNOW it will be painful. It seems easier to cover our eyes and ears and pretend everything is okay.

The road outside of my bolted door has been a shock to my system. In a split moment realization I have had to face that I unbolted the door, yes. Yup. I did. I shattered the silence of my terrible shame I had carried. But, I have also now unearthed more fossils of my past. This is just the beginning. I can't miss a step. I want to, trust me. Instead of 'Do not pass Go and do not collect $200' can I just PASS go and skip ahead to the end of the board game of Life? And in my heart I hear a resounding NO. If I want complete freedom for myself and generations to come, then this road I must travel, all the way to the end. And THIS is why I have so much more to heal from, so I can share it with you so you will know you are not alone; you are understood. There is something mysteriously liberating about being understood.

I can see now though something I never considered. We have to be spilled out or ripped open for God to use us! If I never tell my story, then I never can comfort someone who feels alone in their story. If I don't let myself feel all the feels, where will empathy for others' pain be born? Maybe this is where I begin to live out the words I spoke in faith, while I was initially facing my 'spill'. *"You will do everything You have promised; LORD, Your love is eternal. Complete the work that You have begun."* (Psalm 138:8) MY part is just to keep walking forward.

"I don't want to run from pain.

You know I can't afford to cheapen grace.

I know that pain just means my soul's awake.

"I wanna see Your heart

Through my younger eyes.

I wanna hear Your voice

In the rain and wind.

I wanna know it's safe to be

A child again."

("Child Again" by NeedToBreathe)

For all of us facing any truth of a painful secret or a hidden burden, it IS much like having a surgery. The truth WILL set you free. And it WILL hurt while you heal. But, you did it! Cheers to YOU. As you travel your own road less traveled, may all the shame and blame and pain RIP as you get your life back, little by little, step by step. (RIP - rest in PIECES, shattered and never to be seen again.)

CHAPTER TWO
The Trauma of Re-traumatization

~What I did NOT anticipate was how difficult it would be to break free from what I had carried around with me for over 50 years~

After writing and publishing my first book, I became the not so proud owner of high anxiety. And let me tell you, I did NOT see this coming, though really in hindsight I guess I should have. I mean, really - did I think I would be dancing a jig, lassoing the moon, and grabbing onto a new lease on life in the blink of an eye? Hmmmm... So let's talk about anxiety because, well - it is a very real thing that many people suffer from.

The psychiatric definition of anxiety is: *"a nervous disorder characterized by a state of excessive uneasiness and apprehension, typically with compulsive behavior or panic attacks."* (Wikipedia) In passing I mentioned my newfound anxiety to my grand-daughter whose college major is psychology - I guess I was secretly hoping for an instant diagnosis without sharing any details. Well. I actually got one. She instantly recognized what was going on inside of me, and she said, *"You are being re-trau-matized!"* It clicked right away that she had nailed it right on the head! I looked up the definition - *"Re-traumatization occurs when a person re-experiences a previously traumatic event, either consciously or unconsciously."* (Wikipedia) Whoa. I had NO idea this would or could happen, thus why I am here NOW telling you. My anxiety came from my trauma rearing its ugly head.

In my last book I talk about the years I was unable to cry, and wondered exactly why I was like that. I just NOW remembered that indeed I DID cry during those years of abuse. Just not at opportune times I guess. No one knew from whence came my tears. I cried at night with my head buried in a pillow and no one knew. However my Sunday nights at the altar of publicly sobbing like I murdered someone, I guess did not do what I might have hoped to accomplish. I was surrounded by adults in those years but I do not remember any of them taking me aside to see if I actually needed help. No one looked a little deeper or stayed just a minute longer. NO blame is intended here; I am just showing that the abused are among us and too often they go unnoticed. Eventually I became mechanical. I changed (to cope), and thereafter would not cry or fall apart or allow myself to show the effects of my shame. I did this for weeks that turned into years. As it became my buried secret, all those painful and shameful feelings were buried with it. Year after year after year though, it was slowly but surely oozing out through the cracks, as I talked about in my first book. That was a lot of trauma to bury. That was a lot of emotion to never let out. Thus, why it has reappeared NOW with a vengeance.

When I finally let my soul scream out, all those suppressed emotions and all that buried pain escaped too - like the ghosts of my past showing up with an evil agenda! I found myself unable to handle simple things like - interruptions, noises, bright lights, loud music, group settings, parties. I felt like everyone was looking at me, talking about me, sizing me up, secretly mocking me. I would make plans and cancel them. I wouldn't answer my phone. I would sleep too much, eat too much or not at all, cry too much, shake too much. I wanted to run away. I also have wondered why the past few months I have been more prone to headaches. After I share deeply with someone, or write extensively, or pray desperately my HEAD HURTS and I feel like it's gonna BLOW! I GET IT! The trauma of abuse had rewired my innocent mind to darkness, and NOW the light is bursting back in. Bright light ALWAYS hurts. (whoa)

So now all those suppressed traumatic feelings from my teenage years were now present and accounted for. And I had NO idea this would happen. Makes sense though - of course it would happen. I was like a shattered version of Pandora's box, unleashing all manner of misery upon my own self.

Now what?

THIS is where I have been living the past few months - in the land of NOW WHAT? What is supposed to happen now? How do I banish my ancient ghosts clear into hell? How do I stop feeling like I don't belong anymore? How do I find peace in this storm that I took a nose dive into? How do I deal with being re-traumatized by the abuse I so carefully hid? How do I handle feeling very 'off' in my own skin?

Perhaps the unhealed version of me simply didn't even allow me TO feel! I kept anxiety at bay, pain at arm's length, fists clenched, walls up, all systems GO if it got too touchy-feely in my emotions. Nope. Did NOT appreciate the deep feelings. Why? I had no intention of diving into the deep to see what was there, and so I spent years fenced behind my own barricades.

Until now. Until there is this new and improved healing-in-progress version of me.

And, cue the words - I feel very 'off'.

Somewhere between pain and purpose, is the middle ground of OFF. I was going to describe it as weird, but weird means unearthly, so NOT that but weird also can mean just strange and unusual. So, YES - that! I think it is just the newness of the experience - I let go of my past, what I had dragged around for decades hidden from view. Now, I don't. I let it go, like a balloon up and up and away into the sky, at some point never to be seen again. Except for though the balloon is gone, I am still here watching it slowly disappear into the clouds - stuck in this moment or this middle ground. Maybe THAT is what the location is - the middle ground. Hmmm.

It's funny (or not) that this NEW version of me that I don't totally recognize, I am not fond of all the parts of her yet. What is UP with THAT! (I guess the operative word there is YET.) Does that just mean I was comfortable in my own familiar state of being? Like, when you have slept on a lumpy mattress for SO long, the new luxury foam one takes a minute to get used to. I literally sometimes am having a hard time re-processing things with the NOW me. Before I would have known what to do, which would probably have been to ignore it all and move on in oblivion. Haha NOW? I feel like it is necessary to linger longer, to explore the possibilities, to speak up immediately, to go down rabbit holes, and possibly to OVER think. Geez. I also have discovered NEW parts that I really welcome - come on in and stay awhile please! JUST letting you know that this could be a thing - your **new** you needs time to get acquainted with the **old** you, and see what parts stay and what parts go and what parts get a do-over.

This isn't meant to be deep or profound - but more I am just letting you know that after you heal from anything, there is a transition time. You can feel wobbly on new replaced knees or get headaches behind your eyes from a new glasses prescription. Healing changes whatever was broken, and to get from point A to point B is going to take a minute, so just realize you might feel off - weird - it might seem strange - it may look unusual and unrecognizable. Just keep going. You are transitioning from unhealed to healed, and it is a BIG deal. But remember - I'm gonna be okay; you're gonna be okay.

Every day I live within the results of my having kept that lifelong secret. It wasn't just that it was a shameful secret but more that because I never dealt with it, it altered me from the inside out. As I have said before I live in the confines of my own unintentional failures. I live with endless regrets and things that were negatively modified because of my inability to live my life honestly and as a whole, functioning person. I can not escape THAT part. I wish I could, but ME changing does not mean every part of my life changed too. Flowers didn't instantly start blooming in the desert - I still live in the desert. This for me is simply a reality check. When I hear the saying, *"You can do hard things"* - for me it is a call to action. Present day action. Something I need to do right NOW. So what is my HARD right now? I think for myself I need to define that - call it out - examine it - see if I can alter it or change it.

Well, first I guess I will start with this -

"God grant me the serenity

To accept the things I cannot change;

Courage to change the things I can;

And wisdom to know the difference."

(*"The Serenity Prayer"* by Reinhold Niebuhr)

It comes down to this - you just have to resign yourself to the facts and to the things that will never change. It is my optimistic nature to always look for the bright side - I am the 'glass half full' person. I think I became that way as a survival tactic, and - it worked. But I know through living a pretty long time now, that there are SOME things that just are what they are, and are NOT the sweetener to a glass of unsweetened tea. I am trying hard to embrace the things I can NOT change. But also not be crushed under their weight. My mom's infamous quote - *"Adjust, and carry on."* All the truth - simple and commanding. Do it. **Adjust** - Alter or move to achieve the desired result. **Carry on** - Keep going, continue!

Really though, this right here is the ONLY way to proceed when your life has been uprooted and the pathways are new but the old came along for the ride. You MUST learn to distinguish between what can be changed and what can not. And beyond that I think the KEY word in that little prayer is GOD. This journey to healing from the past and stepping into a new day is realizing what lies in the middle ground - and that there is NO way to do it without God.

"When the best of me is barely breathin'

When I'm not somebody I believe in

Hold on to me

When I miss the light the night has stolen

When I'm slammin' all the doors You've opened

Hold on to me"

("Hold On To Me" by Lauren Daigle)

Sometimes in this journey I find myself feeling too exhausted to continue. Inside of me is this endless struggle of - I'm going to make it! I'm not going to make it! I HAVE to make it! And, repeat. At times like this, I just hit pause. I will do this healing journey like I do everything else - one step at a time. THAT is key to remember. Some day you can travel a mile or two or ten, but other days it may just be a couple steps. Or even just one. Don't despise the days of one step. Just remember to *"adjust and carry on"*. Just keep going.

I heard this quote from a sexual abuse survivor on a tv show today - it was the end of her painfully honest interview; she gazed out over the crashing ocean waves, and simply said, *"All little girls grow up."* I felt that. As simple as that sounds, it hit the same chord in my heart as this line from Demi Lovato's song "Warrior" - *"There's a part of me I can't get back; A little girl grew up too fast."* But THIS time not in an earth shattering, shameful/ painful way - this time it feels like the road to closure.

CHAPTER THREE
Rising From The Depths

~Facing and exposing your hardest truth is the ONLY thing that gives you the green light to proceed with joy and peace and purpose into your waiting future~

We are each a sum total of our experiences in this life. We can even grow used to difficult/hard/painful/shameful paths, and when released from it, return to it - why? Because it might be all we have ever known. We might have NOTHING else to compare it with. It is familiar to us; we recognize it. Shielding it, feeling doomed to repeat it, and covering it seems easier than calling it out and destroying it, because - well, maybe we fear destroying ourselves in the painful process. Maybe we unintentionally even take a role IN destroying ourselves.

Apparently through the years, I had adjusted and adapted and locked myself into a bondage that felt secure to me. Secure means: *"fixed or fastened so as not to give way, become loose, or be lost."* (Wikipedia) If it's all we have known then there comes that **delusional** secure feeling. 'Oh, I know this! I have been here before! It feels right; it feels familiar.' Bondage basically means slavery or oppression. WHY would we EVER feel secure in a situation like that? Why would we choose oppression? What if THAT is all you have known? It's a proven fact that some homeless people, if given a house, would eventually go back to the street, because it felt safer. The new house was scary to them - a risk, the unknown, the unfamiliar. Breaking free is scary business! It takes more strength that you never knew you could muster up, and it has to start with resolve to NEVER retreat.

I won't lie – I have not totally mastered this whole concept; I am ever a work in progress trying to leave the past behind, as well as decipher between what is truth and what is lies.

It is so degrading to see yourself as the cowering victim held in some sort of soul captivity to your abuser. It is so degrading to be attracted to the very thing that worked so hard to destroy you. The attraction is to the familiarity. It is just literally weaved into the fabric of your soul. Sometimes I can still see myself being satisfied with the crumbs from those who trigger my insecurities. I feel like when I was being abused, that every time it was another nail in the coffin of my soul. Like, no escape. I am healing, yes - but I still feel the nails. Sometimes they seem dug too far in.

What brings me the most pain is what is in between the lines of my words; the blank spaces no one knows; like my life's narrative written with invisible ink that you can't see, but it is there. I am living in the consequences of my 55 years of silence. What I held captive within escaped and grew into a giant monster that I am no match for. At least THAT is what it feels like.

Abuse, war, jail, homelessness, abandonment, and illness are just some of the many oppressive things people have faced. They can break you down, change you, and become places in your life where you get stuck. They legitimately could have been injustices, or consequences, or 100% ludicrousness. And if it happened long enough and affected you deep enough, it could be a place you are comfortable remaining. It really isn't because you like it, enjoy it, or wouldn't want to have something better or different. It has just become all you have known. It can feel safe without actually being safe at all. And then, it just becomes like the proverbial hamster running in circles on a ball with no end to the circles - CYCLES! A cycle is: *"a recurring succession of events or phenomenon that usually leads back to the starting point."* (Wikipedia) BAM! As the saying goes, "Pete and Repeat were sitting on a fence. Pete fell off. Who was left? Repeat. Pete and Repeat were sitting on a fence..." You get my drift.

We might have resigned ourselves to our own captivity; we can actually become fastened to our own bondages, and stuck in our own cycles. Captivity is "the state or period of being held, imprisoned, enslaved, or confined." I was taught this truth of having security even in our bondage. I mean, remember the Israelites? How they had been treated so poorly in Egypt? God delivered them and when the journey out got rough, they wanted to RETURN to Egypt. What? Egypt - where they were forced laborers and had to make bricks from straw. Whyyyyy would they wish to return? Well, in their words - *"We remember the fish we ate freely in Egypt, along with the cucumbers, melons, leeks, onions, and garlic."* (Numbers 11:5)

In essence, they were now just hungry on their hard journey out of captivity. Hungry. So they remembered the ONE part of their bondage in Egypt that had brought them security/ pleasure - possibly joy - food. Wow. We could laugh, but don't we do that? I definitely have! We try to find an excuse to 'go back' instead of forging forward through the hard stuff to get to the good stuff.

Perhaps it can be almost compared to an addiction. When we hear the word addiction we immediately think of drugs. By definition addiction is *"a biopsychosocial disorder characterized by compulsive engagement in rewarding stimuli despite adverse conse-quences."* (Wikipedia) This then would hold true to, oh - just about ANYTHING that we engage with because it brings us relief or security or pleasure or even just familiarity, DESPITE the fact it is bad for us or self destructive (like self harming our soul), or just plain ole' wrong.

Ah, self harm. When we think of self harm first we would naturally think bodily self harm, such as cutting. The actual definition is: *"the act of purposely hurting oneself (as by cutting or burning the skin) as an emotional coping mechanism."* The part that stands out to me most is that it is an emotional coping mechanism. This ties the physical deeply with the emotional. Reasons why people self harm are caused from the trauma from abuse - physical, sexual, and emotional. First of all, it is needful to know and believe that it is NOT ever a good idea to inflict pain on yourself. Treating what caused the trauma IS the desired conclusion. This process/treatment will probably look different to every individual person but the goal is the same - get help for what makes you want to hurt yourself.

People physically harm themselves trying to maybe send out a message they can't put into words, or trying to make their pain SEEN when really no one can see it. They could be trying to punish themselves for their own failure or lack or because they think they deserve it. Self harming makes them feel in control somehow/even if just over their own present suffering. I have heard it said from people who self harmed - they just wanted to FEEL something. I feel like there are definitely those of us who do this to our souls. We are indeed our own worst enemy.

While I have never cut or tried to mutilate/destroy my physical body, I have come to wonder if I DO self harm in other ways - like to my heart and soul. IF it is similar to bodily mutilation, then maybe it is also an emotional coping mechanism. Do I set myself up to be rejected? To be left out? To be intimidated? To be last? To fail? To be undervalued? Do I do all of that to myself? And if so, WHY?

For so long I had lived in the confines of my secret shame and all the lies that came with it - the lie that had told me no one wanted to know my secret - that it was way too late to change anything now - that I was too broken - that I could never feel normal - that I could never find innocence again - that I should have told sooner - that my story was history - that justice could never be done - ALL the lies. And I camped there - for decades. It was my unsafe safe place, where I was building my life on shifting sand and unstable ground.

"Do not give dogs what is sacred; do not throw your pearls to pigs. If you do, they may trample them under their feet, and turn and tear you to pieces." (Matthew 7:6) The nature of a pig is that they don't see value in anything. They take and they trample. Pigs don't care that they crushed and pulverized a pearl. Hmmmm, a pig takes and tramples and crushes. Perhaps we could say an abuser has the attributes of a pig. Perhaps we could say that pigs are by their sheer nature, narcissistic. Perhaps we have unwittingly taken up residence in a fenced in pig pen.

Perhaps we feel we can never rise up from having been trampled down.

Oh, but just UNTIL. Until you stand up taller and stronger than the abuse and the abuser. Until you find your own value and worth. Until you walk right back to that moment when they destroyed you, and take BACK your string of pearls! Until you dig your way out of the filthy pigpen. Until you break the cycle. THEN you get to RISE from the depths. THEN you get your life back. Facing and exposing your hardest truth is the ONLY thing that gives you the green light to proceed with joy and peace and purpose into your waiting future.

"And I'll rise up

I'll rise like the day

I'll rise up

I'll rise unafraid

I'll rise up

And I'll do it a thousand times again."

("Rise Up" by Andra Day)

CHAPTER FOUR
Breaking Free

~Part OF healing IS being caught off guard by things you never knew or never realized, or never knew you needed to understand – in order to heal further~

In figuring out what bondages we feel fastened to, I want to stop right here and discuss 'soul ties'. A soul tie is *"a connection with someone deeply embedded into your soul"*. (Wikipedia) Soul ties are created when we feel bound to someone or something; it generally refers to intimacy (sex) but I believe it is us being tied to anything that keeps us bound. It also could be a good soul tie or a bad tie – there is always the good and the evil. Soul ties are formed when there is a physical relationship – or spiritual – or just even emotional. You may feel uncontrollably connected to them. It is someone or something you have invested yourself into, as being significant to your life – again, a good or a bad bond is formed. So, (deep breath here) sexual abuse can form a soul tie with the one who sexually **abused** you.

Being as blunt and authentic as I can without being too revealing, I want to briefly expose something I uncovered about myself. And it was NOT a warm, fuzzy moment. It was a horrible moment of admission for me – I realized one day that I had loved my abuser. THIS caught me so off guard – this was AFTER my initial healing from my past. Part OF healing IS being caught off guard by things you never knew, or never realized, or never knew you needed to understand – in order to heal further. This was one of those things. In asking myself over and over WHY I never told on my abuser sooner, I **finally** understood why. My abuser had ownership in my soul - my corrupted intimacy with him bound me to him, and in some warped, dark way (being all I knew) I loved him. Maybe not a pure love or something beautiful - more something like what I am referring to as a 'soul tie'. This is painful and deep, and I hope not to trigger anyone - I just felt like when I experienced all these things on my own road beyond MY bolted door, I had no manual or therapy per say. I am still on a solo journey learning, fighting, researching, and struggling to NOT give up, so writing the hard stuff out became my way to help myself heal, and hopefully to help you, the reader.

I recognized that the way my abuser left me feeling was worthless, buried in shame, covered by secrets, emotionally drained. It became my normal. I lived there in its shadows. And, I even found myself drawn back there to those feelings. This was SO hard to admit but was part of my healing after the healing. (when I say hard, I mean hyperventailing hard and sticking my head in the freezer to catch my breath hard.)

One of my favorite childhood movies is *The Christmas Carol* (written by Charles Dickens in 1843), the story of Scrooge who was a horrible man who DID change and break the generational curse. In his own childhood, there was this moment where he was left alone at his boarding school at Christmas. You can feel his loneliness and despair. And then THIS - his loving sister bursts through the door happily exclaiming, *"Father is so much kinder than he used to be, that home's like Heaven! He spoke so gently to me one dear night when I was going to bed, that I was not afraid to ask him once more if you might come home; and he said Yes, you should; and sent me in a coach to bring you. And you're to be a man!"* Through the years of my life, I waited for that day to happen. I waited for my abuser to call for me. That never happened, and he eventually died. I realize now that this non-closure has been a driving part of me. I have longed for something that never would or could happen. And I further betrayed myself by remaining silent in my shame. Why?

Let's revisit the Biblical story of Tamar, from my first book. She was raped by her half-brother and her first words to him afterwards were basically a cry **not** to make her leave. What? How did I miss THAT? *"But Amnon wouldn't listen to her, and since he was stronger than she was, he raped her. Then suddenly Amnon's love turned to hate, and he hated her even more than he had loved her.* **"Get out of here!" he snarled at her.** *"No, no!" Tamar* **cried.** *"Sending me away now is worse than what you've already done to me." But Amnon wouldn't listen to her. He shouted for his servant and demanded, "Throw this woman out, and lock the door behind her!"* (I Samuel 13:14-17)

I really have to think on this. So, Tamar was raped. Wouldn't you think she would have wanted to go running out the front door, screaming into the night about the violation done to her? NO. The shame was TOO much, and she clearly felt in that moment she could NOT handle THAT! So she begged her rapist NOT to send her away. He not only threw her out into the night, he bolted the door shut behind her, THUS the title of my books. THIS is the key/this is the reason/this is the WHY for all of us who have been her - who have been tossed out into the darkness of shame.

In that moment of violation, you become one with your rapist. There is a perverted bond there that will never go away. In a sick, twisted way Tamar wanted to STAY with Amnon - even throwing out the idea that they could marry and make this evil right. What on earth? This confusion she had in her mindset, has caused me to examine my OWN mindset, back then and now.

There is a part of me that feels it will never be completely healed or settled - it is the part that feels cheated - that feels like I never got closure, much less an apology. My abuser never sent for me. I never saw him pay or even suffer for how he ruined MY life. I never got to scream out in anger and have him see the pain and rage in my eyes. I wandered the earth for over 50 years with my unhealed broken heart.

A dear friend said to me, (with tears and gasps of anger) after reading my first book, that they wished they could go dig up the grave of my abuser and unleash fury on the decades old bones. That may sound graphic or cruel, but in that moment, I experienced something that was life changing for me. It was the ONLY time I ever felt validated - like FINALLY someone shared MY deepest level of pain.

But at this point what even makes all of this truth to anyone else, when you didn't see what he did to me, or what it did TO me? What makes me feel I can go on, when upon opening my bolted door he was not standing there for me to unleash on? I understand Tamar saying that sending her away was worse. Wait though - worse than what? Worse than staying his victim? The shame on the outside seemed worse than the abuse on the inside? How and WHY is this so?

Have you ever heard of "Stockholm Syndrome"? This is important - we all need to 'get this' - *"Stockholm syndrome is a psychological response. It occurs when hostages or abuse victims bond with their captors or abusers. This psychological connection develops over the course of the days, weeks, months, or even years of captivity or abuse."* (Wikipedia) The key word is BOND, from the word 'bondage'/ slavery. Bond means to have a connection with or be joined together - it is interesting to note this is achieved through an adhesive substance, pressure, heat, and chemistry.

I can pretty much see ALL of those defining words in an abusive relationship. You can bond with your abuser or captor - OR your abuse or your captivity. The bonding is created by responses to behavior. As simple as I can say it - a victim can be groomed to put up with bad to get something considered good - like a reward, words of what feels like praise, or a pat on the back sort of thing. For a child it can be as easy as candy. Thus, why mothers teach their children to NEVER take candy from a stranger. Sadly though, it isn't always a stranger who offers up crumbs of nourishment. Crumbs. Really, that is all you get - so little but yet it feels so filling to your void. Then sadly you can grow so used to it, you are actually lost without it. As it progresses, the victim will continue to accept the bad for the little bit of good to follow. Most humans want to please others because we measure our own worth by the opinions and responses from others. An abuser plays on this empathetic part of his victim. Somehow a victim believes he or she is making the abuser happy, even at his or her own expense. Just to receive a positive affirmation is enough to get rid of any negative thoughts that would hold him or her back. It is abuse on repeat, and the **repeat** is what you become bonded to.

Breaking free of the bondage from a soul tie is going to be a personal journey. Bondages people face are nothing to underestimate and will absolutely look different for everyone. I wouldn't presume to offer a cliche' or glib answer or solution as a "one size fits all". These are just general ways to fight against things that drag us down or hold us back. It may require intense counseling, medicines, desperate praying, journaling through your feelings, creative outlets, setting boundaries, relocating, leaving behind the toxic people, and bravely changing things in your life that have kept you in chains. Whatever keeps you bound, needs to be broken off of you. The best way to do this is to just start; one step at a time and one decision at a time – no matter how small.

I think the very first and most important thing is figuring out if you ARE in bondage to something; oppressed by something or someone. It took me a lifetime really to see what held me down and kept me back. I had to face that the abuse had tainted and warped my self view. For me, writing has been my safe place and my refuge. As I write, I heal. Chains fall off as I face them, look at them, and allow them to fall off. This is now my secure place that I am fastened to.

Regardless of the outward circumstances formed against me, I can be FREE on the inside. I will continue to fight this battle, and win. Galatians 5:1 says, *"It is for freedom that Christ has set us free. Stand firm, then, and do not let yourselves be burdened again by a yoke of slavery."*

I wonder if we return continuously to something that sought to destroy us, why would we do that? There can be something that pulls at you - maybe in your darkest hours, someone or something filled a void. It became like a saving moment or a point of reference or a ray of sunlight. You crave that still. Just like the Israelites and their onions. We KNOW we were abused but the onions were so good. We KNOW we were so lonely but the words "you are beautiful" were so comforting. We KNOW we wanted to be free, but we also wanted to keep our private stash of treasures. Maybe this was initially Lot's wife's dilemma - she had to just RUN for her life, from the city which was destroying her and her family, and was ultimately about to kill them if they did NOT run. Something back there drew her attention - something she longed for - maybe thought she needed or couldn't live without - something she had a soul tie to. And so as we know, she turned back - and she perished for that split second decision. And THAT is her legacy - albeit a cautionary one. We MUST not return to our captivity. We MUST plod on and forget about the onions. (No onion can be THAT good.)

I am also learning to stop labeling myself AS a victim. Victim has a couple ways to define it; "*A person who has been attacked, injured, robbed, or killed by someone else; a person who is cheated or fooled by someone else; someone or something that is harmed by an unpleasant event (such as an illness or accident).*" Of course someone who is sexually abused IS a victim of harm and unmerited assault. How I am no longer a victim is simply because I am NOT. I am no longer in the clutches of harm. **I am no longer a slave to a crumb trail. I am no longer defined by what has hurt and shamed me.** I have found the strength to rise up and proclaim, enough is enough. Therefore, I am no longer a victim! The goal of healing is freedom. Remember that. That is your endgame.

"I am no victim;

I live with a vision.

I'm covered by the force of love,

Covered in my Savior's blood."

("I Am No Victim" by Kristene DiMarco)

CHAPTER FIVE
We Don't Talk About The Big Bad Wolf

~In order to be prepared or aware of predators, we need to recognize them by their sheer predator nature~

In the new 2021 Disney movie *"Encanto"* is a catchy song that has reached number one status - the title is: *"We Don't Talk About Bruno"*, written by Lin-manuel Miranda. Here is a catchy phrase from it…

"We don't talk about Bruno; no, no, no!

We don't talk about Bruno.

Don't talk about Bruno, no!

(Why did I talk about Bruno?)

Not a word about Bruno. I never should've brought up Bruno!"

I am sure those words in and of themselves conjure up a thought of something or someone we do not mention, much less talk about. I was always deeply troubled by **the big, bad wolf** in Grimm's fairy tale of *Little Red Riding Hood*, and like Bruno, I didn't wanna talk about him. And then in my teens there was a rather bewitching rock song titled the same, where they turned the fairy tale into something rather seductive - like danger was enchanting. I decided to go back and revisit the story, the song, and then research wolves. Because after all, wolves are predators and their animal nature is much like the nature of human (sexual) predators. Same thing really. And maybe this is ultimately why I did NOT like the story or the song. I could relate to Little Red Riding Hood. It was right there - all the things I didn't wanna talk about.

First of all, Red (we shall just shorten her name) was referred to in the tale as being innocent, as all children are. Her mother asked her to run an errand - to take some food to her sick grandma, so off she went. On the way she was noticed by - yup - the big bad wolf. He stopped her and asked her where she was going - she straight up told him - I mean, remember, she was innocent so why would she have any suspicions? She had no idea he was dangerous. After easily manipulating Red to give up her plans, the evil wolf went directly to grandma's house, and well, he ate her grandma. I guess I knew that part of the story, but reading it again I was like, whoa. That wolf went from 0 to 100 in a flash - evil knows no bounds, does it? It will do what it wants, to get what it wants. Remember that. Finally, Red got to grandma's house, only to discover NO grandma/ just the wolf in disguise waiting for HER, having plotted her demise. Fast forward, he ate her too. (who reads this to their kids?!) All the big, bad wolf wanted was what his nature demanded - a meal. Predators destroy. It is what they do. So many things in this tale bother me, and really - WHY is this a childhood story anyways? It is pretty VIOLENT. Ugh. But it holds so much disturbing truth.

Something I never thought about till just now, is this - you think the wolf just wanted to eat the little girl cuz she was young and innocent and for a wolf, a good meal. But he ALSO ate the grandma. Wolfs are just out to satisfy their appetite - and really, **everyone** is up for grabs.

Seems to me the childhood fairytale went even darker in the song - and actually gives me the creeps. Feeling an internal creepy feeling from someone can be a signal or alert to danger. Just sayin.

"Little Red Riding Hood

I don't think little big girls should

Go walkin' in these spooky ol' woods alone...

So until you get to Grandma's place

I think you ought to walk with me and be safe

I'm gonna' keep my sheep suit on

Until I'm sure that you've been shown

That I can be trusted, walking with you alone."

(*"Little Red Riding Hood"* by Sam The Sham &
The Pharaohs)

Okay, so in the fairy tale we are definitely talking about a wolf. In this song, we are definitely talking about a sexual predator. There it is - right in between the lines - a lot of warnings right there. I have had this experience. I have known wolves in sheep's clothes. The most horrifying part of this is my response TO the wolves. I have never been able to figure out my pull TO them. WHY would anyone purposefully and intentionally befriend a wolf, knowing that under the sheep suit beats the heart of a predator. Perhaps it is just the very nature OF a wolf, to lure, to seduce, to overtake and to take its victim as prey. Often we blindly and even willingly walk right into the trap.

In the animal kingdom we define a predator as *"an animal that naturally preys on others."* (Wikipedia) For example, lions, bears and wolves are predator animals. In the human kingdom we define a predator as *"a person or group that ruthlessly exploits others."* For example, *'A sexual predator is a person seen as obtaining or trying to obtain sexual contact with another person in a meta-phorically "predatory" or abusive manner/the same as how a predator animal hunts down its prey, so the sexual predator is thought to "hunt" for his or her sex partners."* (Wikipedia)

So in order to be prepared or aware of predators, we need to recognize them by their sheer predator nature. First of all, it crosses my mind that Red's mother should have done that errand herself, well aware that the woods held the likes of a wolf. Perhaps if Red's mom had even warned her young daughter of the big, bad wolf maybe she would have screamed or hit him with a stick or at the very least, RUN for her life. I don't know. I don't blame her or the mom. I blame the wolf. I just see here NO foreknowledge of the wolf lurking in the woods. We MUST have knowledge of predators in order to keep from being their meal. This might seem uncomfortable to reflect upon, but no one talks about it. We have to teach our children about what is OUT there in the woods. If we don't, no one else will. No one told me. And that is why I am here now. I am telling you. Good to note that the innocence in Red was similar to what was in her grandma - a weakness to exploit. Remember in the story her grandma was sick in bed. WHICH means she was weak and at risk. Both were harmless and unable to defend themselves. When we are not prepared, we become easy prey. Evil is no respecter of persons. I can NOT say it too many times - KNOWLEDGE is a weapon. Arm yourself with it. Equip others with it! Tell your kids. Tell their kids. Tell your friends. Tell everyone. Yes, the woods (the world) is a wonderful place with flowers and trees and sunshine and butterflies, but also - evil lurks. And we MUST know this and pass on that truth to the unaware/innocent/harmless generations yet to come. There really ARE big, bad wolves.

The most disturbing thing I read when researching wolves was how generational they are, even in the animal kingdom. Read and shudder, and then you will understand WHY we

MUST shatter the silence and break the curses, and decimate the lies and secrets for the generations yet to come.

"In the wolf kingdom the young wolves watch the behavior of the adults and see how the game is played. They witness how the adults change their strategy according to conditions and type of prey. They learn how the hunters handle each different situation: what to do when the prey dashes for open ground, or jumps into a river, or turns to defend itself. When juvenile wolves finally join in the hunt, they imitate the more experienced wolves and perfect the precise skills of herding and tackling. By the time they are full grown adults, they have become part of a well-oiled machine. Even if they were able to communicate verbally with each other during the hunt, it would be unnecessary. They know exactly what to expect from the others and what is expected of them."

(Wikipedia)

(You should re-read that again. And read it out loud and let it sink in.)

Down through the ages the wolf has become a symbol for a warrior, a wanderer and yes, a killer as it forms and leads a threatening and predatory group. We see this in the wolf in this fairy tale - he is a predatory killer - ravenous in his hunger, vicious, shrewd and cunning. Jeremiah 5:6 describes a wolf as a wild animal who will ravage (severely damage) his prey. At the end of the fairy tale, the "big, bad wolf" is then transformed into the mythical werewolf, thus revealing the utter depth of its evil nature. Yikes. SO much truth in folklore.

I researched the wolf a little deeper and found that the wolf WILL be tamed in the millennial reign of Christ. Wait. What? *"The wolf and the lamb will feed together, and the lion will eat straw like the ox, and dust will be the serpent's food. They will neither harm nor destroy in all my holy kingdom"* (Isaiah 11:6) This describes predator and prey living in harmony with each other. Whoa. (Like a return to Eden?) The thing I get from this is that NO wolf (abuser) is beyond the reach of the hand of God to transform a life. We don't like to consider that - especially when we have been the one abused - we hope the abuser 'gets theirs' and we don't want to even consider they could be saved or redeemed. I guess right here is where *"the rubber meets the road"*, and if we *"have ears to hear"* we can hear the song of redemption ringing out from the heavens - willing to change the predator to one who can become a predator no more.

The ONLY way to break this evil predatory nature in humans IS Jesus. We are born into a fallen world. You could say earth is the woods, and the devil lurks in it as the big, bad wolf. God sent Jesus to be the ONLY one with the power to break generational behaviors, sin curses, and things we unknowingly and unintentionally keep passing on, because we don't deal with them. In knowing Jesus personally and pursuing His ways, we are then able to clearly decipher between good and evil. The chance is offered to us ALL to be clean and pure, passing on nothing evil. THAT is my goal.

"I don't need to recognize

The man in the mirror

And I don't wanna trade Your plan

For something familiar.

I can't waste a day

I can't stay the same

I wanna be different

I wanna be changed

'Til all of me is gone

And all that remains

Is a fire so bright

The whole world can see

That there's something different

So come and be different

In me."

("Different" by Micah Tyler)

There comes a glorious day when the victim finds their voice and their once perceived weakness turns to authority. This is where the roles are switched. The abuser becomes the weak one, and the abused - the strong one. Shame no longer defines you. The authority is found in two parts - first, demanding back your value - secondly, taking away an abuser's power over you by forgiving them. The power of forgiveness is for YOU. It is the secret weapon of your authority now. Then, you get to turn around and walk away. I no longer am consumed by my non-closure and an apology I never received. I am walking away. I feel this in the depths of my soul.

Interesting to note that in Grimm's fairy tale, YES the wolf ate little Red Riding Hood. BUT even though THAT should have been the end of her story, THIS is the rest of what happened - *"Little Red Riding Hood is promptly devoured after remarking "What big teeth you have, Granny!"* **But** *a lumberjack later cuts open the wolf and saves the girl and her grandmother who are miraculously still alive in the beast's stomach."* (Wikipedia) A lumber**jack** saved future generations. Whoa.

SO - in true fairy tale form there WAS a happily after after - even GRANDMA was rescued! Let your own imagination discover any hidden truths here. (For me, thank you JACK Channell - for rescuing me and miraculously keeping me alive so I could get to the here and now!)

If you are reading this chapter (and you relate at all) and you are holding a secret shame that maybe you fell prey to 'in the woods', please - do NOT wait as long as I did to expose it. No one should carry the shame of abuse into the years of their life journey.

Knowledge, preparation and prevention is key for future generations.

The road to grandma's house needs to be well lit, with posted signs, and all manner of evil given NO points of entry. And NEVER go walking in the dark alone.

CHAPTER SIX
Fatal Attraction

~Like a moth drawn to the flame, we are strangely attracted to what feels familiar. Beware~

On this road less traveled, let's stop and talk about moths. Wait. Did I say MOTHS? Yes. Moths. Like bees, they pollinate flowers and plants. Pollen is in essence, plant sperm, and bees and moths are carriers of this. It is interesting to note that bees tend to zero in on the most fertile pollen sources. But moths? **They leave no plant or flower behind.** (Sounds like Marines.) They actually pollinate plants unattended by the bees. Think about THAT for a minute. WE as humans can certainly learn from their unbiased way of treating others. They don't pick and choose who they should help. Their purpose is their purpose, and they embrace it without reservation or complaint.

Next, moths work at night – by the light of the moon. How cool is that!? Moths are part of the lifegiving process by their pollination, and plants that receive pollination are then able to reproduce. The goal of EVERY living thing is to reproduce. For example, moths use the moonlight as a compass, but because its light is so far away it demands that the moth stays in a straight line pattern. The moon is symbolic of eternity and immortality (think on THAT for a while). With such an important job in their bug DNA, how do they end up **dead** in bug zappers? Like a moth drawn to the flame, we are strangely attracted to what feels familiar. Beware. It really is the whole moth drawn to the light concept – **fatal attraction.**

The light that moths attract to is **artificial**, such as the flame of a fire, light bulbs, and the death sentence of lighted bug zappers. One theory surrounding this is NOT that they are actually attracted to it, but more that they are **disoriented** by it. To be disoriented means to be confused. Oh man, do I identify with THIS! A confused moth doesn't know where it is going and loses its sense of direction. The more disoriented, the more the artificial light becomes all-inclusive with a **hypnotic** effect. Artificial light heat radiation imitates *"Moth pheromone-chemicals released by insects to attract mates."* (Wikipedia) Because artificial lights confuse a bug's navigational system, they must focus on the light of the moon, or they are entranced in the glow of the artificial light.

So as a human, how to escape this moth fate? The moon – let's say that is symbolic of the light/nature/heart of Christ. Jesus said He is the light of the world and if we follow Him we will NEVER have to walk in darkness (John 8:12)). He is our steady one, who keeps us steady on in our own night seasons. You could say He is our LIGHT on. Keep your eyes on the true light. Jesus IS the light of the world. Don't let artificial lights fool you (even the expensive ones, the LED artificial lights…) It is either pure light, or it is not. There is NO in-between.

He tells us not to look to the right or to the left. Don't pay any mind to the artificial lights along the sidelines. They will fry you or eat you. So to speak. *"Let your eyes look straight ahead; fix your gaze directly before you. Give careful thought to the paths for your feet and be steadfast in all your ways. Do not turn to the right or the left; keep your foot from evil."* (Proverbs 4:25-27) All those shining, glowing, captivating beautiful lights that call out to your inner self that are prone to preferring the artificial to the real, need to one by one be avoided. *"Let your Yay be Yay, and your Nay be Nay."* (Matthew 5:37)

I was horrified to realize I am attracted to 'like kinds' of my abuser. At first I saw my attraction as part of my healing or some sort of freedom. More and more I understand that yes, I AM healing - and yes, I AM more free than I ever have known before in my life. However, in the freedom of healing, I am drawn to what feels familiar. I already understood the whole security in bondage thing (got the t-shirt). I did NOT understand that the pull to an abuser would be a thing. No joke. I mean really - come on, who is drawn to the same spirit they just escaped from. Um, that would be me. Anyone else?

I DO understand now it is less about the abuser, and more about the SPIRIT behind it. It is very possessive, and when I cut it off it decided to morph itself into more attractive figures. Without details because, who wants that - I have found myself pulled to danger. It is why I wrote about moths - I AM that moth. I have experienced the pull of the bug zapper. And horror of all horrors, I KNOW it, and still I have proceeded.

There was an old rock song by Elvis Presley that says - *"It can't be wrong, if it feels so right."* And THERE it is. That navigational confusion sets in, and we justify the pull or the attraction or the distraction. It feels good. It makes me feel the freedom that I never knew - the healing that I longed for. BUT I don't think feeling good is always a feeling of feeling GOOD like how we think. First let's look at dopamine - *"**Dopamine**: Often called the "happy hormone," dopamine results in feelings of well-being. A primary driver of the brain's reward system, it spikes when we experience something pleasurable."* (Wikipedia) Wait. How can we be drawn back to something abusive, like it gave us well being. Well? In some ways it did - if you were trying or hoping for the love or affection of the abuser, that abuse was attention - though be it all wrong. You got used to it. You aimed to please, whether intentionally or unintentionally, and the reward was the moment of acceptance or simply being acknowledged by your abuser. It becomes part of your brain's reward. THIS is the confusion of the navigational system. It is NOT good. It is like a switch up - the abuse has tricked you with another form. The familiarity is actually creating a false sense of that dopamine - much like the fake light is NOT the true light of the moon for a moth.

Somewhere along the line, I realize it was me - I caused this. No one else to blame - can't blame the bug zapper. It is just doing what bug zappers do. I took my eyes OFF the pure, true light of the moon (Jesus) and decided I knew enough now, after being healed and set free from shame - yeah, I knew enough now to discern between what is real and what is counterfeit. I think I DID know, but I chose the counterfeit because it gave me that sense of danger I was craving - I mean, I am healed now. I am craving some danger. Uh oh. THERE it is. So, yup. My fault.

In owning this pull back, I am hoping I can help someone else who is battling temptation. It is NOT a sin to BE tempted (thank God), but you can only entertain the temptation for so long, before it could become the actual sin. The bug zapper will always be a bug zapper - it will not and cannot be more or less than what it is designed to do. Note to self. NO other light will satisfy more than the one, true light.

God help us as humans to learn to be strong enough to just flip some OFF switches to the artificial lights. Delete. Block. Extinguish. Annihilate. Slay. As we embrace our truest purpose, we will become wise enough to CHOOSE pure and authentic, and be abhorred (disgusted, turned off) by the artificial.

Finally, I think it is really a matter of the heart – to choose Christ. As a result, my own similar purpose (like a moth) is to focus on the Light (Jesus) to serve my purpose in the night season; the season where I pollinate flowers. As I said earlier, the goal for EVERY single living being IS pollination, which simply means creating offspring for the next generation. WE DO NOT LIVE ONLY FOR OURSELVES. I don't want my legacy to be – on her final descent she flew head on straight into a bug zapper. Not when the light of the moon is still there, has never moved or changed, and will lead me home. And I can lead generations home too.

Ironically, my favorite thing to say to my grandchildren is the phrase *"I love you to the moon and back"* from a children's book titled *"Guess How Much I Love you"* by Sam McBratney. I didn't realize all the generational truth in those words. Keeping my eyes on the light of the moon.

CHAPTER SEVEN
Learning To Crush My Fears

~Whether I let fear be my driving force or not is what determines the quality of my LIVING~

To be afraid is a controlling emotion caused by feeling SURE that something (or someone) is a threat in some way, or will cause pain or even be dangerous. Do you realize that every day you leave your house, you are taking a risk with your life? It isn't just that you could catch a deadly disease if someone coughs on you, or another car could side swipe you on the driver's side, you COULD get killed crossing the road in front of your house just checking your mail. In fact, I fell IN my house, in my own bathroom, missing slamming my head on three different hard surfaces in front of me by mere inches. I could have died on my own bathroom floor! (NOT what I would want my obituary to say...cause of death/hit head on toilet bowl.) Point being, living IS risky business. Whether I let fear be my driving force or not is what determines the quality of my LIVING! Another thing to keep in mind - fear is a LIAR!.

"Fear, he is a liar.

He will take your breath,

Stop you in your steps.

Fear he is a liar.

He will rob your rest,

Steal your happiness,

Cast your fear in the fire

'Cause fear he is a liar."

("Fear Is A Liar" by Zach Williams)

I realize my ability to emotionally grow up was stunted - stunted means to be prevented from growing or developing to full potential. Until you finally face your fears born from abuse or injustice, you can emotionally remain at the age when it occurred. I feel like I never completely grew up until, wow - the past few years. Yikes. In some parts of me it feels like I was 15 for 50 years. So guess what - as I have been healing I have revisited ALL those desolate, barren, scary places. I did NOT realize I just needed to call them out, identify them and crush them.

As I have revisited the various stages of my life lying dormant, it has indeed felt like I picked up where I left off. I could see where I had never fully progressed emotionally. I now understand why I have adversely reacted or responded in some of the ways I did. The crazy makes sense. Fear was implanted in me at a very young life - so young that indeed, it became a part of me I never invited to stay. For instance, when the fearful child in me resurfaced (only long enough for me to call it out and deal with it) I had reactions to other people as if I WAS that fearful child again. If someone dominated over me back then, I felt it again - certain personalities triggered my fear. I felt cornered, threatened even by people who would never do me any harm. Make any sense? I really thought I was losing my mind ever so slightly. NOW I get it. Just those triggers that I am now guessing I will keep experiencing all the way till the end of my healing journey. The thing is, they come when they want to - out of nowhere, triggered by something from the past.

With each trigger I identify and call out, the stronger and more alert I become. **Fear loses its grip on me**. Darkness has to run for cover! Oh yeah! The fearful child and beaten down teenager finally gets to stand up and grow ALL the way up. I know now that I can't hope to help anyone else until I can help myself. I need to solve my own mysteries, unlock ALL the doors, uncover my own skeletons in the basement, look my demons square in the face and let the healing waters rain over me. I have lived one minute too long being controlled and manipulated by fear. *"So, first of all, let me assert my firm belief that the only thing we have to fear is fear itself — nameless, unreasoning, unjustified terror which paralyzes needed efforts to convert retreat into advance."* (1933 Presidential Inauguration/Franklin D. Roosevelt)

These little triggers of fear remind me of spiders. I am scared of spiders. I do NOT like spiders, and don't try to tell me - oh, it is just a tiny one. Nope. A spider IS a spider. All the fearful 'what ifs' about spiders. (insert a shudder.) Currently living out in the country - guess what. LOTS of spiders. I stay on 'spider alert duty'. Crush. Kill. Destroy. I may or may not have stomped a visibly dead spider into dust, because - you know, just making sure he WAS dead. The mighty shaking in her boots spider warrior! So, I can forever be traumatized by their lurking presence in the corners, just out of sight. Or - I can search them out and crush them! But also I can almost sort of co-exist with some of them. They are NOT going away, right? A spider is always about 8 inches from each of us, at all times. Sorry to tell you that fact if you were not aware of it. Maybe we could look at emotional triggers that way? I can search them out - and then destroy them, as I am able. And for some other things, it is just life. They are just going to be there and I have to deal with it. I may just need to hit pause, step back, and take a deep breath - call a spade a spade, and walk on. Rise up and activate your own strength. Remember, at the end of the day you will ALWAYS be bigger than any spider - even the biggest and baddest.

"You're my courage when I worry in the dead of night

You're my strength 'cause I'm not strong enough to win this fight

You are greater than the battle raging in my mind

I will trust You Lord, I will fear no more."

("I Will Fear No More" by The Afters)

What decimates fear? TRUTH. I must drop 'truth bombs' on the fears which translate into lies, every time they raise their ugly head - which sometimes is every single day. Maybe that is why God said we should hide His words in our heart - His words are truth, sharp as swords so like a weapon to fight with. Ah, so when Satan whispers I shouldn't have ever been born, then he gets THIS response back from me - *"The Lord called me before I was born, while I was in my mother's womb He named me. He made my mouth like a sharp sword, in the shadow of His hand He hid me; He made me a polished arrow, in His quiver He hid me away."* (Isaiah 49:1-2) TRUTH bomb dropped dead on the lie - BAM! Decimated! I am emboldened by the thought that God knew my name before I was named. And the fear has to GO! (Bye bye fear - please let the UNBOLTED door hit you on the way out!)

CHAPTER EIGHT
I Am Unraveling

~Healing the core of who you are is THE most important thing you can do for yourself~

To unravel is to "*undo twisted, knitted, or woven threads*". (Wikipedia) It is an unwinding of what was tightly entangled or knotted. Voila' - **ME**! Unraveling is part of my healing, even maybe a BIG part. I MUST unravel. But boy, it is scary and unfamiliar and many times I hear myself saying (to myself) WHO are YOU!?

In my unraveling I discover new parts of me I never knew, or parts of me I have never experienced, and parts of me that were never allowed out. I feel like one big knotted and twisted braid, wrapped up so tight that there wasn't even room for a bird to make a nest in the braid. In my unwrapping, there are a lot of ta-da moments. I can go from shocked to angry to surprised to happy to embarrassed to devastated, all in a matter of hours. I can also feel daring enough to run down uncharted paths simply because I feel so FREE inside! I am traveling rugged terrain I've never ventured upon. All my suppressed feelings that lay dormant for 50 years are all standing at attention now. They all demand some sort of attention, and each one is saying - HEY! Notice me!

I have always had parts of my life I couldn't remember. Either because of trauma or just time moving on; I really didn't know. I had prayed if there were things I needed to recall, that I would be able to, when I was ready. Or, maybe better left forgotten. I had a feeling they were dark in nature. And I knew in my gut that whatever I couldn't remember, I had forgotten for a reason - maybe unintentionally on purpose. I say unintentionally because when you're a child, what do you actually know to be good or bad, or true or a lie - you just upload and store. It is all there, people. All the things. All the memories. And only God can heal the damage from the abusive ones. I filed those under UNDISCLOSED SECRET. However, my inner child has finally shown up on her own behalf. Man, it took SO long for her to get here - so sorry younger self that I held you captive.

"I keep fighting voices in my mind that say I'm not enough,

Every single lie that tells me I will never measure up.

Am I more than just the sum of every high and every low;

Remind me once again just who I am because I need to know."

("You Say" by Lauren Daigle)

Seriously God - please remind me just who I am! It is almost like all those stifled teen years of hiding behind my lie, have come out of hiding now - and I am 65 feeling like a recycled teenager. Woohoo! FREEDOM! The new found freedom has also shown up with fleeting feelings of recklessness - Uh oh. What? You're kidding me, right? Reckless means: *"Impulsive, daredevil, unthinking, wild…"* (Wikipedia) Yikes - sounds like any normal teenager I have ever known (and raised!) THIS has been hard to deal with - it is like the young person in me has emerged full of vim and vigor - ready to go, but there is now nowhere to go. I shudder to think that in a different situation I might have chosen to be reckless, and so easily! THAT is what has shocked me - how easy it has felt to feel like I would dive off the deep end had there been one. YIKES. My logic knows that we are NOT set free to be free to do what we want or to fulfill our fleshly desires. I somehow want to be able to feel free without also feeling reckless. There seems to be a fine line.

Freedom by definition - *"the power or right to act, speak, or think as one wants without hindrance or restraint."* (Wikipedia) So when we can finally operate without hindrance or restraint, uh oh. Oh the choices! Oh the temptations! I think all of us who need to heal, are currently healing, or have yet to heal NEED to know what lies ahead that may come with NO road signs or GPS - just all of a sudden there may be a deep crack in the road and we could go right in.

It is as if NOW I am ready to be a new (normal) wife, a mother who understands her role (to be parent and not friend) - the two jobs which are gone; over; not redoable. This has brought immeasurable sadness to me, and regret. And frustration. As I have said before, it is like finally showing up to a party you were invited to - and you are so late that everyone has gone home. In fact, you are SO late that there is NO sign there ever WAS a party - the silence is deafening and the cobwebs are visibly noticeable.

I now feel completely different. You feel completely different once you open your bolted door and let go of the past. In fact, I am not even completely sure WHO this new version of me IS. Like, am I really different, or am I who I should have been or was meant to be? Or, just different because healing demands it.

As I began journaling over the past few years, it really felt like my story started writing itself and I was the unwilling author. But the more I let out, there came a time when there simply was NO going back. I was shattering my own silence - first to myself, now to everyone else I guess. The hardest thing I ever did was to say the words - *I was raped!*

As I have stood face to face with my younger sexually abused self, something in the total definition of the word *rape* jumped out at me - "*taken with or without force, without the consent of the victim. an act of plunder, violent seizure, or abuse; despoliation; violation: the act of seizing and carrying off by force.*" (Wikipedia) Whoa. I feel like we generally describe a rapist as someone who violently or forcefully takes his prey. And yes that is very often true. But also THIS - "*without force*" shows manipulation to cause someone to feel they HAVE TO give in to the abuse, and then THAT triggers their guilt and shame, because they feel they accepted it willingly and knowingly. (So much truth.) **THAT was me.** Just embracing this now helps me no longer define blame myself as if somehow it was my fault. **It feels like all the knots in my soul are slowly unraveling.** I heard these words in a television news interview today, which resonated loud and clear to me: "*Fight for innocence.*" (Jessica Howard/ USA Gymnast) Innocence was stolen from me and now I am fighting for it for others to be able to keep, and/or find again - like me. Healing the core of who you are is THE most important thing you can do for yourself.

It is a fearful thing to look back and see yourself having been so damaged. It makes me feel like - why was I even born? Maybe I shouldn't have been. I DO hear that lie. It feels true. And yes, I know it IS a lie, but it feels legit. These are the moments when I have to consciously decide NOT to give up, and not to quit.

"Darkest water and deepest pain,

I wouldn't trade it for anything.

'Cause my brokenness brought me to You,

And these wounds are a story You'll use.

So I'm thankful for the scars,

'Cause without them I wouldn't know Your heart.

And I know they'll always tell of who You are

So forever I am thankful for the scars."

("Scars" by I Am They)

An injury to your body (or soul) will most likely always hurt to some degree, if it was a serious injury, and yes - may leave scars. I had foot surgery last year for broken toes. My foot has never felt 100% and always has an annoying pain when I walk, yet the xrays show it DID indeed heal. Interesting. It didn't return to the perfect, straight, bending toes of my youth. They were way too damaged and broken. All that the surgeon could do was straighten them, put pins in them (the other option was amputation), and warn me that we have no way to know how this is going to go. Speaking of how amputation was on the table for an option, let's see the actual definition. *"Amputation is the removal of a limb by trauma, medical illness, or surgery. As a surgical measure, it is used to control pain or a disease process in the affected limb, such as malignancy or gangrene."* (Wikipedia) Maybe sometimes we DO require that but it clearly seems it is a last resort. So my toes continue to hurt/ not in a debilitating way, but more just a reminder of sorts to 'proceed with caution', and it keeps me very aware of my steps. For me what matters most is, I CAN walk. I learn so much about the inside of me from the outside of me.

I could just stop right here on my journey to healing and go no further. Sometimes I feel so exhausted from the mental warfare, I just want to quit.

It feels too hard.

You get tired of fighting.

It is lonely on solo journeys. And even if others try to join you, it's kinda impossible for even the most compassionate among them to really understand how you feel. There is only one thing to do when I feel like this - NOT quit. Literally just drag myself around another bend.

"I'm coming apart at the seams

And everyone's pulling at me

And I am unraveling

The smile isn't quite what it seems

But it does well to hide what's beneath

All the pressure is staggering

In the unraveling, Father unravel me

When I can't feel a thing

Have mercy and let me bleed

I know it's dumb

But I have been numb

For way too long

I don't want to be alone anymore

I don't want to just survive anymore

And I want to feel, so unravel me

Yeah

Unravel me

I'm coming apart of the seams

It's worse than I thought it would be,

But I've never been happier."

("The Unraveling" by Cory Ashbury)

So in my unraveling of the past (and the knots in my soul), I have learned that the new biggest thing I personally am battling after healing from past trauma IS the newfound freedom! In this freedom I feel the sting of the past captivity more intensely and deeply, and I feel the joy of being able to move forward more intensely and deeply. Wow. It's funny that the thing I have been searching for, could also be the very thing that undoes all my new progress. Except I am determined to get it right, but NOT without having to choose and pick and decide and discern over and over and over again.

Freedom comes with a price. And the price is expensive, but also priceless.

We WILL learn to navigate through, as we choose wisely, stop and think before acting, and remember why we started this journey. And the newfound freedom is growing from the inside out so it is ALL new to you. It is YOUR unraveling and YOUR freedom walk.

This unraveling IS a good thing and a long overdue thing. The freedom trail is freshly paved and a place you have never been. So, march on but march slowly while you are still healing. IT TAKES TIME. When this whole healing is complete it will be much like when you go to the doctor's and FINALLY you get your bill of health, even if there are scars. THAT is what I am fighting for. THAT is where I am headed.

"When You cried out from the garden

Let Your will be done, not mine

When You took the weight of my mistakes
So I don't have to fight 'em
Now I let the sun rise on every scar and every sign
Of when You took this bruise and dying soul."
And breathed it back to life."

("Undone" by Kim Walker Smith)

CHAPTER NINE
Face To Face With Myself

~I am not defined by my imperfections; I have now become more valuable BECAUSE of them~

Anxiety has been such a new thing to me. I am not sure I totally understand it - at all. All the years of trauma and abuse that I endured, I do not remember identifying myself as having been anxious. Or was I? Did I just suppress it? Did I ignore it? Bury it? Cover over it with my loud mouth? I compartmentalized the pain; I shelved it. I have been told I WAS painfully shy and reserved when I was very small. I think I went from painfully shy to the other extreme during and after abuse, to hide or cover my timid self. Maybe back then I adapted a loud, fearless version of myself as a front/a disguise. It was like a costume I wore so you couldn't see what was underneath. And I wore it so long that it became form fitting. I even fooled myself. Until, I took it off. And I became who I am seeing today. Oh dear. I don't recognize THIS version.

Looking back at my suppressed trauma is helping me understand the high anxiety I NOW feel towards - just about anything! Really. No heads up or warning - just anxiety and sheer panic mode. Like, don't talk to me - don't look at me - don't ask me for anything. I feel like I am not enough/can't be enough/can't do enough/ I clash with the light and with noise and with life in general. THIS is what I refer to as my "road less traveled" - I may have tiptoed on it through the years, but this is my first time charging down it in an old beat up Ford truck.

Anxiety is defined as: *"A mental health disorder characterized by feelings of worry, anxiety, or fear that are strong enough to interfere with one's daily activities, Examples of anxiety disorders include panic attacks, obsessive-compulsive disorder, and post-traumatic stress disorder. Symptoms include stress that's out of proportion to the impact of the event, inability to set aside a worry, and restlessness. Treatment may include counseling or medications, including antidepressants."* (Wikipedia)

Something I have had to deal with in myself is that part of the definition that says *"stress that's out of proportion to the impact of the event."* Yup. That is ME the past few months. Everything looks huge to me, even very small things. I have learned this is the result of all the anxiety I suppressed for so long - all the ways I faked my way through - all the times I retreated into some hidden or subliminal land of make believe. I could not deal with reality so I suppressed the emotions I had never learned to express or even acknowledge. SO much of why I write these books is so that YOU will know what I did NOT; so that YOU do not have to walk the same roads I did, or for as long as I did. More often than I care to admit though, I say these words, "I can't do it anymore." But then, I do. For myself and for YOU, I press on.

Coming face to face with myself in real time recently looked like this - So, by way of a marketing consultant I paid money to email blast a couple thousand people an announcement about the release of my book. I heard back from 6 people, whom I then sent books to for review. From there I heard back from, no one. I thought - oh wow. THAT was a big mistake and a waste of money. And I won't do that again. I was half disappointed and half relieved. But then lo and behold 3 months later ONE radio DJ contacted me back, for a radio interview - thus, interview no. 2 with a complete stranger, who by the way was a man - and just the fact that THIS did NOT bring me anxiety in and of itself, is a GOOD sign. I mean, really? A man to interview me on my story of sexual abuse. Whoa.

I was nervous, but not anxious - big difference. The DJ was very kind and a well seasoned interviewer. During the interview I came to this moment when I realized he was 'going there'- he was about to ask me what my book was about/what happened to me. Like, the bottom line. In my head I was prepared to say I was a victim of sexual abuse - a nicely padded answer - but what I heard come out of my mouth was, "I was raped."

OH my GOD. I heard myself say the three words that had ruined my entire life; the three words that apparently now I had spoken out LOUD which I did NOT intend on saying. So, I kept going. I finished the interview. As I hung up the phone, I immediately felt the anxiety raise its ugly head. I realized what I just did. And, I got an instant migraine which lasted about 6 hours. I thought about calling him to delete it. He would have, sure. That really would have been no problem, and no big deal. Except. In the midst of my anxious thoughts, I also was like, I SAID IT OUT LOUD! And, so easily. Words I could never speak just rolled off my tongue. And straight into the atmosphere. I didn't know if I was happy or mortified. Eventually, and after a couple close friends cheered me on - I finally felt like, okay. I guess I am GLAD I said it. My best friend said to me, *"Maybe just ONE person needed to hear you say that!"* I grabbed onto her words like a lifeline. So, in all actuality - beyond the written words in my book saying I was raped, my own actual voice finally shattered the silence! My secret has been decimated. And, if it helped ONE other person, it was worth the 6 hour migraine. And, you know what? Really, it DID help one person - telling My own story helped ME! It helped me go a little further into exploring a part of my life I never spoke of.

How I am feeling right now reminded me of a chapter I wrote in my first book titled - "The Golden Repair", comparing God's grace to the Japanese art of Kintsugi. I wrote about it then because at that time I was just newly facing my own brokenness and needing God's grace to fix me or make me new. Today though, it feels different. Today I got it to the depths of my soul. Today I realize I have lived out the meaning behind the art of Kintsugi.

"As a philosophy, kintsugi is similar to the Japanese philosophy of wabi-sabi. an embracing of the flawed or imperfect. Japanese aesthetics values marks of wear from the use of an object. This can be seen as a rationale for keeping an object around even after it has broken (whoa!) and as a justification of kintsugi itself, highlighting the cracks and repairs as simply an event in the life of an object **rather than allowing its service to end at the time of its damage or breakage.***"* (Wikipedia) There is a theory that kintsugi started when a damaged Chinese tea bowl was sent in for repairs in the late 15th century. When the tea bowl was sent back, it had been repaired with metal staples, so NOT appealing to look at, and this may have inspired other craftsmen to find something more acceptable or pleasant. It became its own new art form, and somewhere along the lines it was discovered that valuable pieces of pottery could actually be repaired with gold threads called kintsugi. The ugly became beautiful, as well as more costly. The cracks had made the broken pottery MORE valuable as it was reinvented/remade instead of being tossed aside as trash. Wow. I get it. That is me.

I have struggled with the realization of how many people in my life who were treasured parts of my journey, knew me only as a cracked pot and may or may not ever know the repaired version of me. It took my breath away actually, and made me cry. All the people - all the years - all the inner turmoil and undiagnosed trauma I disguised so well, so I thought. Except it came spilling out in dysfunctional ways most of them would NOW understand. Ugh. Oh my heart. I am guessing I would present SO many aHA moments - like, OH now we get it. Teenage friends. College roommates and friends. Churches. Friends. Family members and friends now passed. Even my beloved husband. And then there's my own children who knew me broken longer than they are now knowing me whole. Whew - this is a lot to speak of.

So, all of those people who knew me broken? All the regrets I feel because of that? It has been a lot to face, but FINALLY I can see that I have actually become more valuable because OF my brokenness. I am not defined by the cracks or the imperfections, nor by my abuse or my anxiety. If I could get THIS truth out there, that healing does THIS, then it is worth my pain of this discovery. I literally can NOT go back and fix what was broken through those decades - if I could time travel, I would. God knows I WOULD. But I cannot. So all I can do is go on from here and realize I have been on the Potter's wheel and I have been remade. The cracks you see NOW have real authentic light shining from every single one.

"I've heard You can take what's broken

And make it whole again.

Well, here's the pieces of my heart;

What can You do with them?

'Cause I can't hold them all together anymore.

So I let them fall surrendered to the floor.

Only You can bring such beauty

From the depths of all my pain.

Only You can take this shattered heart

And make it beat again.

Oh, You hold us all together in Your hands.

I surrender all I have and all I am.

You make all things new.

You make all things new.

God of mercy and love,

Do what only You can do

And make all things new."

("He Makes All Things New" by Big Daddy Weave)

I remember when someone texted me some really thoughtful, good solid perspective on my anxiety - I remember I just replied back - "Thank you. I feel understood." So, if YOU feel broken and beyond repair, then I hope right now you also feel understood. I can assure you God makes all things new. I am face to face with myself - the newly improved ME, and I can see where the ugly has been turned to a thing of beauty.

I shed a lot of tears writing this chapter - if you are looking at me NOW, **I** am your sign. There IS hope for every broken soul to be made new.

CHAPTER TEN
Stop The Bleeding

~Jesus spoke healing and freedom and hope to not only the woman with no name, but to women everywhere~

The woman with the issue of blood. In history she has no name. Deemed the most unclean. *"Now there was a woman who had been suffering from hemorrhages for twelve years; and though she had spent all she had on physicians, no one could cure her".* (Luke 8) *"A hemorrhage is "an escape of blood from a ruptured blood vessel, especially when profuse."* For 12 years her own uncleanness made her untouchable to and from others. Can you imagine feeling like that? Or, have you ever? She sought to be free, to be healed, to be clean. Basically, she was bleeding non-stop and all over the place, for 12 years. Her condition was a constant reminder to her day in and day out of the depravity of her very existence. How utterly sad. She is me. The woman with an issue of blood - in my soul.

"I just let go

And I feel exposed

But it's so beautiful

'Cause this is who I am.

I've been such a mess

But now I can't care less.

I could bleed to death

O Lord I'm ready now.

All the walls are down

Time is running out

And I wanna make this count...

Lord I'm ready now

I've nothing left to hide

No, no reasons left to lie

Give me another chance..."

("I'm Ready Now" by Plumb)

I think you can have a bleeding issue in your soul. Something ongoing, unattended, and debilitating. Therefore I can now identify myself with this woman. She had been bleeding so long it became a part of her. She walked down the street, bleeding - year after year.

BUT then she heard of Jesus.

After all the doctors she had seen who could do nothing for her, I love that she dared to take a risk - a step of faith, in essence for what she did next. *"She came up behind Jesus and touched the fringe of His clothes, and immediately her hemorrhage stopped. Then Jesus asked, 'Who touched me?' When all denied it, Peter said, 'Master, the crowds surround You and press in on You.' But Jesus said, 'Someone touched me; for I noticed that power had gone out from me.'"* (Luke 8)

Let's backtrack to when Jesus said, "Who touched me?" Anyone who has ever felt shunned, abandoned, cast down, abused, and broken would always be waiting for the other shoe to drop or their one moment of insane courage to be instantly stripped away. I would have thought - oh no! I shouldn't have touched Him. He thinks I am not worthy. I am NOT worthy! He didn't mean to heal me! This was all a big mistake! How could I think He would heal ME?

Fast forward to when she spoke up - STOP. THIS is so significant to me. Jesus basically was calling her out to BE her own hero and stand up for herself. Wow. She really could have turned and ran away, disappeared into the crowd WITH her healing. But she stood up, stepped up and "came trembling". This shows her fear. I wonder if she thought Jesus would take back her healing if He realized WHO He had healed. Why was she scared? Because when you have been that broken, being healed is a scary thing.

But she pushed through - through the crowds, through the scorn, through her physical pain, through her mental anguish, through her fear, and in spite of bleeding everywhere to get to Him.

"If I but touch His clothes, I WILL be made well." Immediately her hemorrhage stopped; and she felt in her body that she was healed of her disease," (Mark 5). She KNEW she was healed.

She touched Jesus and then others, because she had nothing to lose by daring to believe that the impossible might actually be possible for her. Jesus not only healed her but He pronounced a blessing over her life.

"I pray for your healing

That circumstances will change

I pray that the fear inside will flee in Jesus name

I pray that a breakthrough

Would happen today

I pray miracles over your life

In Jesus name."

("In Jesus Name/God Of Possible" by Katy Nichole)

He spoke healing and freedom and hope to not only the woman with no name, but to women everywhere! To me! *"Daughter, your faith has made you well; go in peace, and be healed of your disease."* (Mark 5)

In thinking a bit more about this woman, I more and more find myself identifying with her on a secondary level. First, it was just more symbolically feeling her pain of carrying around such a heavy burden which also left behind the effects of it wherever she went. As I said, that is SO me. Now I ALSO see THIS - a blood issue by definition is: *"a discharge, the consequence of uncleanness..."* (Wikipedia) Something unclean causes a discharge? Whoa. Okay, so - I get that in the body. Now let's apply it to our soul - sexual abuse (for me) was the unclean factor of my life and the discharge could be measured by it traumatic effects on me. Oh man, makes so much sense. And helps me stop perpetually beating myself up for my sometimes slow (but sure) crawl towards my full healing.

THE most significant word in the whole story of this woman (thanks Katrina for the heads up!) is THIS - Jesus called her DAUGHTER! Oh.My.Heart. She who was nameless in a crowd, becomes the one He lovingly calls "daughter". This is everything to me, and maybe for you also. He sees us. We are NOT just another face in the crowd or another bleeding soul.

CHAPTER ELEVEN
Pain And Relief Intertwined

~The biggest way I know I am healing is, that I know I am healing. Yes, that is what I meant to say~

In this chapter I will recite some of the great things I have and AM experiencing since letting go of my past. My mind literally feels clearer, like all the cobwebs were swept out. The air smells cleaner - it feels crisper, I think my senses are sharpened or coming back to life or something. Here is my new found relief intertwined WITH my pain from healing. It is quite the oxymoron.

For starters, I NOW can actually rethink and revisit painful times/failures/circumstances/memories and sort through them reasonably without having a melt down. THIS is HUGE. No joke. This is something I never could do. *"Your head knows, but to convince your heart and your gut is more difficult."* (USA gymnast Jessica Howard) Yes. That is 100% true. I avoided any and all confrontation with all things painful by ignoring it or dismissing it or simply not acknowledging it, as I stated in book one. THAT is what got me HERE in the first place.

It is nice to feel normal enough to just be able to thought process my life - all of it - my failures and my successes, the intentional ones and the unintentional ones.

It is a new day. The sun is shining. The trees are in full bloom. The rocks are being carted off; the water is running clear. (That dead cow polluting the waters has been removed.)

This next sign of healing in me is a biggie - my activation to triggers is getting fainter. I still have them and deal with them, but they are losing steam. I can't tell you how MUCH I appreciate THIS part of my healing. I long for the day when any random narcissist has no power over me, not in word or deed, or manipulation or guilt. Maybe I will always have a built in alert system, and that is okay - but now I can identify it and call it out, and not be provoked in my soul. I feel like I am gaining the upper hand.

And then there is THIS effect from my healing journey - I no longer feel consumed with being everything to everyone. WOW. This is a lot. Women, and particularly mothers are nurturers and burden bearers. It is what we do and who we are. I am officially there. I cannot carry all my own burdens and everyone else's in the entire world - or even just my own little part of the world. I embrace the truth that I can not and will not please everyone all the time. My own self imposed soul therapy is closely tied TO the word 'self'. If you need to heal, it IS all about you. Most people that have ever been abused, lean towards the concept of being content as door mats. They are so used to being trampled upon in whatever way/shape or form their abuse happened, that the last person on their list to care about is themselves, or - they don't even make the cut! **I finally recognize my own needs**. It may sound selfish. It is NOT. I am just reversing the effects of low self esteem, and the damage done to me by internal shame. When you start your healing journey away from the dark clutches of shame, you MUST see your own value and embrace your OWN worth. Otherwise, healing is stunted. If you don't see your value, you can't fight for yourself. I was so beat down in my soul from those years that I was devalued and dismissed, that I stopped even thinking about my wants and needs. It is so easy to do that. All the things you learn in church seem to point to sacrifice, taking the low place, and servanthood -and YES, that is all true! We should be compassionate and serve others, but never at the expense of NOT protecting our own worth. Really, how can I help YOU if I can't help ME first? And I think maybe that causes burn out in church people. They do and do and do for everyone but themselves. Well. Guess what? This current healing process requires my full attention to - self. I am learning to just do ME. And THEN I will be able to better serve others with a heart full of compassion and empathy, drawing from my own reserve. There will be enough to share then.

This next one is hard to admit, but for the sake of telling the truth I am telling the truth. I lived most of my life with my own personal stash of day to day secrets. No, not evil secrets /not secretly dealing drugs or something. But just about anything that had any layer of accountability to it spooked me, and I would avoid it or cover it with a phony layer of partial truth. I lived in the shame of my own flawed humanity I guess. This had become a survival skill while being abused which granted me the ability to live that double life, though I wasn't that great at it. Or was I. No one questioned it. Anyways, that is gone from me.

"Truth is harder than a lie

The dark seems safer than the light

"And everyone has a heart that loves to hide

I'm a mess and so are you

We've built walls nobody can get through

Yeah, it may be hard, but the best thing we could ever do, ever do

Bring your brokenness, and I'll bring mine

'Cause love can heal what hurt divides

And mercy's waiting on the other side

If we're honest."

("If We're Honest" by Francesca Battistelli)

I no longer feel any need whatsoever to not admit I ate the last cookie or forgot to pay a bill or overdrew my account or didn't actually agree with someone about something. I am NOT perfect at this yet, no lie (pun intended) but - it is healing in me. Truth, like a flag, is being raised in my life.

And then, there is THIS - since publishing my first book, I have now done two radio interviews. As a writer, words come easier and faster by typing them as they come into your mind, at least it is that way for me. To speak them out loud? Well, that is a bit harder. So beyond the radio interviews which of course, I was anxious about BUT did it - I got the opportunity to be part of a documentary, which is basically a sharing of personal stories. When I said yes, I guess I overlooked the fact that I would have to be seen. No hiding behind book pages or radio waves - this was a face to face with myself. I agreed to do it, then panicked and said No. THEN, I heard a song, of which I will post some of the lyrics. And then you will understand why I changed my mind from a NO to a YES.

"Even the Perfect One

Was desperate to be free when He cried,

Take this cup from me.

Even the King of kings

Felt it just like me.

Kings feel it,

Beggars and thieves feel it;

That down on my knees feeling,

You wanna give up.

You wanna shut down.

You wanna let go.

You wanna check out.

Don't you, don't you...

Don't you quit!"

("Don't You" by Jordan Smith)

I felt a new surge of strength arise in my soul (another way I know I am healing), and I decided to do the hard thing. For me, speaking out the words and then having to view my own face saying them, was MY hard thing. Maybe for others, no big deal. For me though, a milestone. I did it! My granddaughter recorded me. I spoke for 15 minutes. Funny story - I had cue cards and notes, but guess what - the light was so bright in my eyes I could not see either! I had to speak from, well - the right place - my heart. After all, who knows my story better than me? I guess I did not need cue cards. Was it perfect? Nope. Was I awkward at moments? Yup. Was I authentic? Yup. I like to call it by that phrase "perfectly imperfect". THIS my friend - moments like this where before you would have bolted and run, or hid somewhere in fear and trembling - THIS is when you know that healing is happening. Fear loses its grip, as you face it head on and do the hard thing!

71

"*Healing doesn't mean the damage never existed. It means the damage no longer controls your life.*" (Akshay Dubey) The biggest way I know I am healing is that I know I am healing. Yes, that is what I meant to say.

CHAPTER TWELVE
Integrity Takes Courage

~CHEERS to Queen Vashti who has NEVER gotten to clear her own name; she literally sacrificed her CROWN to do the right thing~

In my first writing attempt a few years back, I wrote a short allegory (words that reveal a hidden meaning) called BE YOUR OWN HERO. It was about a princess who was fighting against a fiery dragon; it was about her struggle. It was me - the me trying to raise my silent voice up to a frail whisper. My BOOK became my primal scream, and the dragon has since been slain. I got to become my own hero, but it was too long of a journey - and one I hope YOU will embark upon a lot sooner, if need be. Because *"Silence only breeds more silence. It is a predator in and of itself, equal only to what is being held in secret."* - my own quote from my first book.

First, do you value your own self enough to BE, or to BECOME your own hero? Queen Vashti did and boy, did she get the short end of the stick for it! So it seems…

We talk about the bravery of Queen Esther (as we should), but we have overlooked the bravery of the Queen before her - Queen Vashti, so I have been researching Jewish history about her. She has been frowned upon as the tarnished/banished Queen who wouldn't obey her husband the king. Um. Let us explore that. I offer that perhaps we have NEVER been taught correctly about WHY she was banished.

Vashti means "beautiful" and no doubt was THE most beautiful woman in the kingdom. She herself had been a Persian princess who married a king. He reigned over 127 provinces in India. He was kind of a big deal - at least, clearly in his OWN eyes. In his drunken state, her husband King Ahasuerus demanded her to strip naked for his drunken friends -

"On the seventh day, when the heart of the king was merry with wine, he commanded his seven eunuchs who served in the presence of King Ahasuerus, to bring Queen Vashti before the king, wearing her royal crown, in order to show her beauty to the people and the officials, for she was beautiful to behold." (Esther 2:10,11)

And he literally meant for her to ONLY wear her crown. She flat out refused to be made a spectacle in front of lust filled, drunken men. So, wait. THIS is her disgrace? We have been taught from right here, that she disobeyed her husband and THAT has been ALL we were taught. Her disobedience. I mean, here it is -

"For the queen's behavior will become known to all women, so that they will despise their husbands in their eyes, when they report, 'King Ahasuerus commanded Queen Vashti to be brought in before him, but she did not come.

If it pleases the king, let a royal decree go out from him, and let it be recorded in the laws of the Persians and the Medes, so that it will not be altered, that Vashti shall come no more before King Ahasuerus; and let the king give her royal position to another who is better than she. When the king's decree which he will make is proclaimed throughout all his empire (for it is great), all wives will honor their husbands, both great and small."
(Esther 1:19,20)

His decree sounds a whole lot like the narcissist domestic abuser he was! And the people he had surrounded himself with, fed his greedy selfish narcissism.

CHEERS to Queen Vashti who has NEVER gotten to clear her own name - she literally sacrificed her CROWN, her royal heritage, her good name, and her keys to the kingdom, to do the right thing. She must have known WHO she was inside, and she valued her own character more. *"A wise woman refuses to be anyone's victim."* (Maya Angelou) She was dismissed, dethroned, and disgraced because of it. I found this quote online with no reference to who said it, so I will just credit it as a google find. Whoever wrote THIS was on point! *"Queen Vashti was on point. The king was up to no good. Once Queen Vashti made up her mind, she was ready to deal with the consequences. She teaches us about the role of integrity and courage; integrity takes courage."*

I was thinking how I felt I had no power over myself the years I was being sexually (and emotionally) abused - no power over my body, my words, my decisions, nothing. I don't think I even understood I had a voice or a choice; I remember feeling powerless and victimized. I am sharing MY story in the hopes of empowering YOU to feel courageous to find your OWN power over your body, your mind, your soul - to begin to think, to challenge, to speak, to rise, to walk the road to healing. Like Queen Vashti, WE must see our own value and worth and courageously stand up for ourselves, against all odds, at all costs. I did NOT know how to do this until 50 years after the fact. I had not a clue, and really why I am writing this book. No one EVER can or should tell you that you should have known better, or that it was your fault it happened, or worse that you are a liar when you try to speak up. THIS is the manipulative words used to keep you from flexing your power muscles (so to speak). You must take back YOUR power. In the words of Maya Angelou, *"I got my own back. "* BE YOUR OWN HERO.

CHAPTER THIRTEEN
No Longer Remembered

~For those forgotten girls (and boys) who never got a chance to be heard, in the halls of eternity I hope they each know that we are breaking THEIR silence~

There was that day - the one where a king robs his own kingdom of all the young virginal teenage girls. Let us call this what it was - the premeditated sexual abuse, corruption, and exploitation of young girls from Ethiopia to India. Just exactly how much pride and arrogance can one human have! All I can think of to say next is that king or no king - he was a PIG. I would like to interject here that this fuels my fire to continue to let my voice be heard, for those girls who never got a chance to be heard. I call them 'the forgotten girls' - forgotten by definition is: *"Of which knowledge has been lost, which is no longer remembered."* (Wikipedia) I am bringing them ALL back from their place of being no longer remembered. And in the halls of eternity I hope they each know that we are breaking THEIR silence. *"Develop enough courage so that you can stand up for yourself and then stand up for somebody else."* (Maya Angelou)

I watched a movie on sex trafficking (sexual slavery) which totally wrecked my mind and heart. All I could think of was these girls in the harem of a king. So in essence, he had his own private stash. He didn't sell them to the highest bidder, but he kept them all for himself. To this present day the average age of girls who are trafficked is 14. To think that a precious teenage girl is an object to be used. To only be so consumed with lust as to ruin a life in less than 5 minutes. It is too much to comprehend. *"Human trafficking is an open wound on the body of contemporary society, a scourge upon the body of Christ. It is a crime against humanity."* (Pope Francis) And THIS is the evil backdrop to Esther's story.

Unlikely hero (again) my girl Esther. I still can't shake that there is so much more to be said about her, and FOR her. We tend to see her on her throne, a queen with her crown, who saved the whole Jewish race. All true. But her initial story makes me shudder. Not only an orphan who tragically lost her parents, but snatched from the only safe place she called home with her Uncle Mordecai - in the middle of the night. Snatched. Kidnapped. Trafficked. Stolen teenage girl - ALL the ways to describe her horrific journey before becoming the strong queen we admire so greatly. It makes me also question the whole 'pain to purpose' thought process I often speak of. It makes me really ask God, WHY? Why a kidnapped Jewish girl, sex trafficked to an evil king - THIS was the ONLY way You could see fit to save a people? What I went through in sexual abuse was the ONLY way You could see fit to save a people? And I have learned the answer is first of all NOT simple, but it is a YES. We don't get to question God. We do not understand (nor can we) His ways. He sees from an eternal view. He sees from perfect eyes. He pierces those eyes right through the sin and imperfection of our fallen world, and somehow He DOES take pain and turn it into something of value and worth.

Back to teenage girl Esther, also named Hadassah - *"The name Hadassah is primarily a female name of Hebrew origin that means **Myrtle Tree**. In the Bible Hadassah was the name of Esther before she married King Ahasuerus of Persia."* (Wikipedia) As most of us know, Esther means star. I decided to start with her name, before I even dive into those young years. So her name went from meaning myrtle tree, to star. I want to explore that first - A myrtle tree is the Hebrew symbol for marriage. Hmmmm. It is often said our purpose is in our name. I do NOT think names are random. I think we are meant to have the names we get. Names matter - remember that. After all, God says He knew our NAME in the womb. So, ready for this? The myrtle tree has flowers on it - shaped like STARS. *"Myrtus communis (true myrtle), of the family Myrtaceae, is a fragrant, evergreen shrub with small, glossy green leaves and white, star-shaped flowers."* (Wikipedia) The small tree had to grow for the flowers to appear. Whoa. ALL the truth there. I wondered why her name was changed. I found this - *"Her name was changed to Esther to hide her identity upon becoming queen of Persia. The three letter root of Esther in Hebrew is s-t-r (רתס⬜), "hide, conceal". The passive infinitive is (לרָתְָסַה⬜), "to be hidden".* (Wikipedia) You can't make this stuff up - it is all right there.

So, her purpose WAS in her name. Okay, digging deeper. Without her journey, there was no road to the throne room. She had to walk the path set before her - in all its seeming unfairness and pain. I struggle with this. She was a mere 14 when she was dragged out of her home and into the king's castle, to become part of his harem. Um, yes. Harem. A harem in Arabic means a forbidden place. By definition it means: *"A group of women who are sexual partners of the same man."* (Wikipedia) ALL the teenage girls were dragged off to be groomed to be the king's new queen. I find this gross. Just sayin' it. They were underage. The king was NOT a good person. He was wicked. So, God was about to use an evil man to groom a young virtuous girl to be his. It is like a donut eating contest - which one will be his favorite? I find this so disgusting and it rips my heart out for ALL those teenage girls. Sure, we know the end of the story - but what about all the other girls who did NOT get chosen? In the book of Esther there are only 8 chapters, and you really have to dig deep and think and research, and ponder to read between the lines. You will have questions that can never be fully answered.

It starts like this - let's read the actual account -

"Then the king's servants who attended him said: "Let beautiful young virgins be sought for the king; and let the king appoint officers in all the provinces of his kingdom, that they may gather all the beautiful young virgins to Shushan the citadel, into the women's quarters, under the custody of Hegai the king's eunuch, custodian of the women.

And let beauty preparations be given them.

Then let the young woman who pleases the king be queen instead of Vashti." (Esther 2:2-4)

The only small morsel I can offer in the king's defense is, it wasn't his idea. BUT again, because his heart was evil, he was easily influenced by the wicked counsel that he had surrounded himself with.

As far as I can tell through researching this, there were an estimated more than 300 girls. Can I just say a resounding EW here? I mean, does anyone else read this the way I do? The king tossed out his WIFE (because she refused to do his evil) and now wants a replacement, because - I don't know, he's lonely? Angry? Depressed? Needs a one-nighter with each girl in his harem? Again. EW. Wait. Let us remember too that the king had all the men killed off in a previous war, and now all the single women (um, NOT women) were the object of his affection - like, Hmmm, which one do I want? One more resounding EW.

And somehow God Almighty is going to turn this mess into something meaningful and valuable? Still struggling here.

Still working my way through this, so bear with me as I find us answers, or at least as I find peace with this scenario.

Onward to the king's harem - (I literally find so much discrepancy in historical accounts about the ages of the girls - I read anywhere from ages 14-25.)

"When each girl's turn came to go to King Ahasuerus at the end of the 12 months' treatment prescribed for women, for that was the period spent on beautifying them: six months with oil of myrrh and six months with perfumes and women's cosmetics.

After that, the girl would go to the king, and whatever she asked for would be given to her to take with her from the harem to the king's palace. She would go in the evening and leave in the morning for a second harem in charge of Shaashgaz, the king's eunuch, guardian of the concubines.

She would not go again to the king unless the king wanted her, when she would be summoned by name."

(Esther 2:12-14)

The evil king summoned each girl he wanted by her name. Jesus calls us by our name. (Interesting thought that stopped me right here.) There is something that tugs at our heartstrings when someone calls us by our name. It plants the sense that you are not a stranger to them, and possibly removes a warning if the source is NOT pure. Jesus calls us by our name because He indeed knows us and loves us. For Satan, this is a trap he sets, **as if** he knows us and loves us - remember there is always a counterfeit for the real. Always consider the source. Again, think about it - *"She would not go again to the king unless the king wanted her, when she would be summoned by name."* (just food for thought.)

So, all the girls get their turn when summoned by their name - if their one night with the king is pleasing to him, they could be called back for another round. If not, they are told - keep the jewelry and the beautiful clothes (as a parting gift? A pay off?) and NOW, they are sentenced to a life of seclusion - never to see the king again or to get to marry another man. The forgotten girls. They remain desolate. Sounds a LOT like Tamar, from book one. It rocks me to my core as a woman. I cried a lot for these forgotten girls. There is NOTHING redeemable in this story.

Um, except that there IS. Hadassah. Aka Esther. Let us now return to her story. The evil king chose her, as we all know. The story tells us it was because of her heart. EVEN evil had to bow before goodness. She became the brave queen who then risked her life to persuade him to NOT annihilate HER people, the Jews. God used her precarious dilemma so that HE could do a supernatural, miraculous intervention THROUGH her - you know, God turns to good what Satan meant for evil! Satan only sees as far as the end of his pitchfork and evil plan - he really just doesn't get it - God has the final say and EVERY knee WILL bow before HIM and not Satan. No matter the mess - it is true that God can turn it into something absolutely breathtakingly beautiful.

Esther was SO much more than the oils and the lotions and the gowns and the jewelry. God already knew this, didn't He. He KNEW her heart was perfect before Him, and that SHE could go through this pain with dignity and grace, and that He would raise her up to be so much more than she would have dreamed. Like Esther, we just need to say YES, I will do IT (whatever IT is) - no matter how hard it is, or how scared I am, I will step onto the stage.

Hear the commencement as the Master Conductor lifts His baton and begins to develop a breadth of view for your life. Imagine how that will sound as it joins with others, in a mighty symphony of heavenly purpose. In our own individual lives we are EACH here *"For such a time as this."* (Esther 4:14) Hear that sound in the depths of your soul, and let it awaken you to hope.

CHAPTER FOURTEEN
The Unbroken Grow Weary Of The Broken

~It is a sad moment when you realize that not everyone wants to hear your story, but needful to understand your story is not meant for everyone TO hear~

This chapter right here is about a twist in the road with overlying branches I got tangled in, and had to figure my way out of. Maybe you could call it a side path to the main road. It was not pleasant, but it was necessary to travel down.

It is very disturbing that when you are a victim, you can become the one shunned and set to the side. I have literally felt this since writing my first book. Not everyone will welcome the healed version of you - and nothing has surprised me more. It is like you stand up, and everyone else stands down. I wasn't going to go 'here' but for the sake of others lost in the cracks, I am. Let me just carefully and gently tell you that not every other wants to hear your story. And actually people will get weary OF hearing it. The horrific details are simply too much for them. It is easier and safer to walk away, before hearing too much and then becoming responsible for what you DID hear. Unbroken people grow weary of broken people. Why? Because they are not broken. An unbroken person may look at you incredulously and wonder WHY? Why didn't you speak up? Why didn't you just leave? How can this really be true? You looked so happy; now you're telling me you weren't? And horror of horrors they may even stick up for the actual abuser. Also if it has laid dormant as a buried secret for years, why bother to bring it up now? Let bygones be bygones - get over it - just move on. THIS is the language of the unbroken. They see what they see with their EYES, and what is logical and what makes sense. They may view us as irrational, unsound, unreasonable, and judge our stories as unfounded, over the top, and possibly exaggerated or even untrue. Wow. And God bless them - we who are broken are SO glad you have never walked in our shoes. Seriously. So glad - not being sarcastic. It is hell to be a victim. And further hell to be misunderstood.

I have a friend who is a victim of domestic abuse. I was appalled at the reaction and inaction of most of whom were her closest friends or the circle she was encompassed within. At a time when she is fighting for her life and the life of her family, she finds herself more alone than ever. She is being shunned, whether intentionally or unintentionally; she feels more alone than ever.

First of all, a victim should NOT be further victimized for being the victim. Read that line again - A victim should NOT be further victimized for being the victim.

No one who has endured and survived sexual abuse, verbal abuse, domestic abuse and more - use it as a badge of honor. We don't speak of it (finally) to flaunt it somehow or to make you notice us. We actually don't like being noticed. It is all complicated. It is like - 'look at me, but don't look at me; be there for me, but go away'.

For me, I finally told my story of sexual abuse from so many years ago, to free myself from carrying the secret. That was first and foremost. Then, to dare to believe that the peeling back of the years and layers of shame and destruction, could possibly help anyone else. I have found that yes, indeed it DOES - one person/one story at a time. I am so okay with that process - slow and steady. What I did not expect was for people that know me or knew me when, to go dark. The silence has been deafening. Honestly, I had NO expectations of what the result would be in sharing my story. I only wanted to let others know they are NOT alone. I had no idea what that would look like, or be like, or feel like. I had zero anticipated results. I feel ghosted, shunned, and actually more alone than I did before.

You need to understand why people shun and run. Let's just call it that - 'shun and run'. Shun means: *"persistently avoid, ignore, or reject (someone or something) through antipathy or caution."* (Wikipedia) You know how on a subway you hear a recorded voice over the loudspeaker say - *"Stand clear of the closing doors please."* Well, that is kind of like the thought process of people who can't bear to hear our painful truths - *"Stand clear of their painful stories please."* Right here I want to say - we MUST understand that you can't comprehend what you can't comprehend - they don't understand our level of pain and shame, so they simply can't relate to it and in many cases, are not willing to try. It is too much for them. And this is NOT something for us to take personally. It is what it is. It is a sad moment when you realize that not everyone wants to hear your story, but needful to understand that your story is not meant for everyone TO hear.

If you are reading this as a victim of some abuse, just please know most people DO care; they just may NOT know HOW to respond. It is really that simple. Responding can feel like taking a side or having to get in a mudhole with you (they don't want to), and it totally shakes their own comfort zone. Really - it IS hard to hear OUR stories.

Along the way there WILL be others who though NOT understanding, are willing to just be present with us in our pain. I would call them 'dirt friends' - I like to call them THAT because they are willing to get in the mudhole with you and get dirty, without understanding why, without a word, and with no agenda. Can I just say thank God for DIRT FRIENDS.

But you must realize your **target audience** to tell your story to, are people just like YOU. THEY will get it. THEY will understand. THEY will cry with you. THEY will grieve with you. And THEY will stay with you.

To YOU and you know who you are, remember - Roar.

"Momma's waiting at the finish line

And wipes the teardrops from her eyes

She says, "You did just fine honey, that's okay

Sometimes life's just that way

You're gonna lose the race from time to time

But you're always gonna find

You can't lose me."

("You Can't Lose Me" by Faith Hill)

CHAPTER FIFTEEN
Wildflowers And Cookies

~A warm reaction (a.k.a. wildflowers and cookies) to some-one's pain may matter more than all the words you could offer~

Now I want to speak to those who need to know HOW to respond to those in pain from any kind of abuse, grief, and loss. It isn't always about having the right words. So, first of all stop trying to come up with something profound or meaningful to say. Maybe, it is more about NO words but LOTS of action. Maybe, we don't even want to hear what others think or feel. It might add injury to insult. Maybe that sounds harsh; it is not. It is just the truth. Victims need the affirmation of uncondi-tional love. THIS could look like an apple pie left at the door. Or a card in the mail. Or some flowers tucked in the mailbox. I promise you THIS kind of warm reaction to someone's pain may matter more than all the words you could offer. Words will come later, and maybe MUCH later.

If YOU know a victim of abuse who is trying to stand up and step out, don't go dark. Don't disappear.

When my husband died, it became a solo journey for me emotionally. I went from being the other half of the equation of *"Two shall become as one"* back to being one. And I was still a mother of six kids and grandmother of three. No matter how hard anyone wanted to comfort me, it was almost impossible.

My next door neighbors taught me a very important life lesson. I am adding it in, right here and right now because it mattered so much in my healing journey. For months after my husband died, the neighbor sent her kids walking about a mile to my house. NOT to try to talk to me. Truth be known, I would hide if anyone came to my door. Again, it is that complex - I want you in my life but also, please go away. Every day for months those amazing young children left me things at my door - flowers they picked, notes they wrote, pictures they drew, cookies their mom baked - and then, they would turn around and walk back home, in silence. THIS was my life line. I couldn't reach back to them, but that didn't matter to them - they were just being present, sitting in my dirt pile with me. Just being! While they did NOT have a clue of my pain, they unconditionally loved me. That was all I needed.

Please hear me - I understand if you don't know what to say now to your friend who just admitted to years of abuse, or lost her husband through a painful divorce or death, or can't seem to stop grieving. Hear me - just show up in all the thoughtful choices that lie before you. Be creative. It matters. THIS was 18 years ago, and it mattered SO much that it is going in my book now. It let me know that I was not alone even though they could not join me in my sorrow. It let it be okay for me to hide behind the curtain until they left, then go retrieve their gifts of love. It let it be okay for me to be broken into a half. I needed just to feel the love. And I did. And I remember it all these years later.

So I pray as you read these words that you will comprehend the great love that victims so desperately need, and that it will always be reflected in the very tiny things. Victims on a journey to NOT being victims anymore, are NOT looking for fanfare and stirring words and wailing on our behalf. Just affirmation. Maybe just wildflowers and cookies.

CHAPTER SIXTEEN
Because We All Need Saving

~I'm reminded that we always leave footprints to follow – whether for good, or for evil. So we should make careful consideration where we place our feet~

I was looking in the Bible to see if I could find any other abusers to research if and how they found redemption. As I was thinking along these lines, the name Zacchaeus popped into my mind. I was like, Zacchaeus - wait. Who was he? And why would I think of him while researching abusers. Well, all I knew of Zacchaeus was that old traditional children's song.

"Zacchaeus was a wee little man,

And a wee little man was he.

He climbed up in a sycamore tree

For the Lord he wanted to see.

And when the Savior passed his way,

He looked up in that tree –

And He said Zacchaeus you come down,

Cuz I'm going to your house today."

("Zacchaeus" by author unknown)

I first found it intriguing the kind of tree he climbed up into - a sycamore tree is symbolic of finding clarity. Zacchaeus had to climb it to get a clear glimpse of JESUS.

(Interesting thought process.) OH, and he was a tax collector! All of a sudden, I am also intrigued as to why Jesus was looking to hang out with HIM.

So, I first looked up WHO Zacchaeus was. Being a tax collector in his time was NOT a popular career position to have, and not a way to win friends. He was a social outcast; a cheat - he stole and manipulated and he technically WAS an abuser - he abused poor people by stealing from them unfair and unjust taxes. Tax collectors in Bible days were an in-your-face symbol of oppression. They were hated and called sinners; Jews who worked for Romans, were also called traitors, and rightly so. They took more than necessary, and took what was not theirs. They actually targeted the poorest of the poor who surely could not pay up their debts - why you ask? TO CHARGE THEM INTEREST! THIS is the man Jesus wanted to visit and share a meal with? HOW does he get to be sought after by Jesus? Let me just say this right here - Jesus wanted to have dinner with a known abuser. I really have to process that thought in my mind.

I proceeded to look up the meaning of the name Zacchaeus, which means 'pure' or 'innocent'. Cue the crickets - what? Funny not funny since he was a despised tax collector. How ironic really, and sad - to have such a name you could NOT live up to. BUT wait - let's just read the whole story of what happened that day.

"Jesus entered Jericho and was passing through. A man was there by the name of Zacchaeus; he was a chief tax collector and was wealthy. He wanted to see who Jesus was, but because he was short he could not see over the crowd. So he ran ahead and climbed a sycamore-fig tree to see him, since Jesus was coming that way.

When Jesus reached the spot, He looked up and said to him, "Zacchaeus, come down immediately. I must stay at your house today." So he came down at once and welcomed him gladly.

All the people saw this and began to mutter, "He has gone to be the guest of a sinner."

Let's pause here a moment before finishing the story - First of all, no doubt all the onlookers criticized Jesus for going to the home of a known cheat. I love that Jesus was obviously already looking for Zacchaeus, while it just appears that Zacchaeus was looking for him. Divine appointment? Why did Jesus want to go to a tax collector's house? Wasn't he unworthy? Wasn't he the bad guy? Yes. But. There is a BUT here.

"BUT Zacchaeus stood up and said to the Lord, "Look, Lord! Here and now I give half of my possessions to the poor, and if I have cheated anybody out of anything, I will pay back four times the amount."

THIS! Zacchaeus got to FINALLY find the purpose of his name, and to embrace it. But HOW? If you see this how I see it, you should by now be feeling like - whoa. Jesus clearly sees past the man's sin - and into the man's heart. It reminds me that we always leave footprints to follow - whether for good, or for evil. And we should make careful consideration where we place our feet. Let's remember again that Jesus did NOT come for the ones who do not have need of Him. He came for the lost. Zacchaeus was lost. HE being the abuser was able to be saved, redeemed and purified because first he chose to follow Jesus, and THEN he changed his evil ways, and THEN he made amends to the evil things he had done. I don't think most of us consider that we should fix what WE ourselves have broken, if it is in our power to do so. There are many opportunities for us to apply glue to broken cracks we ourselves created.

"Jesus said to him, "Today salvation has come to this house,

*because **this man, too**, is a son of Abraham.*

For the Son of Man came to seek and to save the lost."

(Luke 19:1-10)

This gives me so much hope to tell others that you are never beyond His reach. The more fallen and broken you feel, the harder He is actually seeking to find you. Why? To save you. Wow. Satan shames us with our failures and our sins and our fallen natures, but God seeks to save us FROM those things - not to condemn us for them. Jesus is ALWAYS the Savior. A savior is someone who rescues another from harm, danger, or loss. That is His whole identity in one word. I think OUR whole identity is meant to be found in Zacchaeus' name also - innocence. We can find innocence lost, whether as the one abused or yes - the abuser. God's grace seeks for us all. Salvation is for us ALL. *"Ask and it will be given to YOU; seek and YOU will find; knock and the door will be opened to YOU."* (Matthew 7:7)

A friend just now reminded me that indeed one of the 12 disciples Jesus chose was **also** himself a hated tax collector - Matthew! Whoa. I mean, let's put that into some cringeworthy words for some of us - Jesus chose an abuser to be one of HIS disciples. HERE is the key to this whole story - Jesus called Matthew to follow Him - He asked him to leave it all behind - bringing nothing of his past with him. **And, he did.** He left his position, his money, his security - and the heavy weight that he carried as one so hated and evil. *"Therefore He is able to save completely those who come to God through Him, because He always lives to intercede for them."* (Hebrews 7:25) Those words - *"able to save completely..."* Wow.

I never expected to write a chapter based on a simple childhood Sunday School song. and cry through the whole writing of it. But I am realizing that my abuser was as loved by Jesus as I am. *"How precious is Your unfailing love, O God! **ALL** humanity finds shelter in the shadow of Your wings."* (Psalm 36:5-7) We all have a choice to make when Jesus calls us. And I find this truth very freeing. I finally feel like I can fully and completely move on. Not a cobweb is left in any dark corners of my soul - in fact, there are NO more dark corners.

CHAPTER SEVENTEEN
Mud Can Become A Place Of Redemption

~Put yourself in the place of the blind man – with your own unique story, but with the same Jesus~

For many years when I was stumbling around in the dark. I was tripping, searching, breaking, destroying, questioning, fearing, as if I was blind and did not ever have a clue where I was going. Except for Jesus. HE knew where I was. HE knew every misstep I took. HE knew every lost moment I would never reclaim. HE knew my every fear and He called them by their names when I couldn't. HE held me until that day – the day when He gave me back my sight. When I was blind and basically used to NOT being able to see, did I hope to ever see? I feel like I had nothing to compare to being blind in my soul – I had been that way for as long as I can remember. I couldn't SEE … yet. Just like the blind man, blind from birth.

And THIS Bible story I have heard my whole life - NOW I get it.

"As He went along, He saw a man blind from birth.

His disciples asked him, "Rabbi, who sinned, this man or his parents, that he was born blind?"

"Neither this man nor his parents sinned," said Jesus,

"but this happened so that the works of God might be displayed in him.

As long as it is day, we must do the works of Him who sent me.

Night is coming, when no one can work.

While I am in the world, I am the light of the world."

After saying this, He spit on the ground, made some mud with the saliva, and put it on the man's eyes.

"Go," He told him, "wash in the Pool of Siloam". So the man went and washed, and came home seeing. His neighbors and those who had formerly seen him begging asked, "Isn't this the same man who used to sit and beg?" Some claimed that he was. Others said, "No, he only looks like him." But he himself insisted, "I am the man." "How then were your eyes opened?" they asked.

*He replied, "The man they call Jesus made some mud and put it on my eyes. He told me to go to Siloam and wash. So I went and washed, and then I could see." (*John 9)

And so there is that. Blind but now he sees! I want to tear this story apart - so much there I never researched or explored or considered. And so much about it that can relate to each of us on a personal level.

First of all, it was not hereditary that he was blind. He didn't become blind because of anything he had done (not a consequence) nor was it his parent's fault. I am guessing they blamed themselves, as ALL parents do when anything goes wrong with their children - we always think it is something we did. And any injustice is attached with blame and shame. Right here Jesus makes it clear - the man was blind and it was not his fault. We tend to judge the flaws in others as if somehow they chose them. Gee, I think I will choose to not have my sight - sounds like a great plan. NOT. Life just happens.

Next, Jesus said there was a purpose (a profitable aftermath) for the man's blindness (the supernatural works of God on display in him). Whoa. Wait. Really? Think about that. So that thing in our lives that is our cross to bear so to speak, can become the very thing that defines us with a purpose and a WHY? For me, sexual abuse? That is deep and intense and troubling really. Okay, keep going. Jesus explains how dark the world is, and how short our time is here. He says that HE is the light of the world and while here on earth, basically He must perform miracles so others will believe - so generations (us) who follow behind people like the blind man, will be reminded of His power to redeem and heal and restore. Basically, Jesus came to be the proof of God. OHHHHHH man, I am starting to really GET IT! My shame from abuse kept me bowed down, face to the ground.

The blind man - okay - how did Jesus heal him? WHAT did He use?

Well, the actual ground where the blind man had stumbled and fell; the dirt he had sat in for years and years. THE SAME DIRT. What had been his place of captivity and shame, became his place of healing and purpose. No longer simply dirt - the ground became the very thing that Jesus used to anoint the blind man's eyes to see! When you add Jesus to any equation (even dirt piles) they become places of redemption.

This is a lot. Go a bit deeper - Jesus spit on the dirt to turn it to mud to put on his eyes. Even the spit of God is miraculous. Whoa.

Okay, moving on. Jesus sent him (with mud caked on his eyes) to the Pool of Siloam. (Aren't you curious what his thoughts were?) The Pool of Siloam was where fresh water was stored, also called the Lower Pool in Isaiah 22:9. *"You saw that the walls of the City of David were broken through in many places; you stored up water in the Lower Pool."* Siloam means *"sent".* (Wikipedia) The even deeper meaning is that the pool was filled with fresh and clear gushing water. And the water was stored there because of all the broken places around it. (Cue the crickets...that is something to really ponder.) Also, being sent to this particular pool gives Jesus' miracle credibility from then to NOW - it is an actual historic location - not something in a story without authenticity or fact. I had to laugh at the reference for this pool's credibility and location - II Kings 20:20. Blind man gets his sight back here - WOW. Right? 20/20 vision. (I explored this in my first book.)

Don't we want OUR stories to be authentic and real, so generations to come will have reason to believe them as truth? Jesus clearly had a plan, from start to finish. At some point we are required to just have that ONE moment when we have some faith in the same Jesus.

Let's back up a minute - Jesus SENT him there. The blind man had to get there still blind, but NOW with hope in his heart and mud on his eyes. His healing was a journey - he had to trust this man - I wonder if he knew it was Jesus or who Jesus was - no, I don't think so, but his heart knew what his mind could not. He was encountering the Son of God and if He said get to the Pool of Siloam, he was going there. I find this significant for me - when I decided to take my journey back to find my own healing, well - it was a choice I made. I felt that pull into the unknown - I know now that was Jesus calling me, just like He called the blind man. I will heal you, yes - I need YOU to do this first, as an act of your faith and trust. And He sent the blind man on his journey - still blind, eyes caked with mud and spit from heaven (so to speak) - maybe this represents all our fears mixed with hope that become our driving force for the healing - and He sent him to a spring of clear life giving water where Jesus told him to wash himself. All the wows. SO deep.

I am guessing the blind man also was exhausted from his travels trying to get to his healing. I can identify with him. My own personal tired is the tired of someone fighting through layers of caked mud impacted in the sands of time. It is the tired of someone who no matter what will NOT stop fighting for herself, and for her bloodline, and for strangers she will never meet.

Why? Because there is something magnificent to be said for finding your place of redemption IN the mud.

Finally, well - there was the miracle as we know it - the blind man was NO LONGER BLIND. Mission accomplished. Jesus healed the blind man with the same dirt he had sat in for years. Same dirt. We may have a different story, but it will always be the same Jesus who comes with our redemption - He comes where we are and meets us there. Even when it is messy and dirty, and muddy.

CHAPTER EIGHTEEN
Just A Walk In The Park

~The beautiful tree grew bent with its imperfections, and as it grew its imperfections became its purpose~

This past summer I went with three of my grandchildren to this quaint little park in Burbank, California, where there is a play area of swings and slides, and there is also a beautiful little tree. It is the most popular attraction in that park because of the shade it offers from the hot California sun. At first I only noticed the thick, lush foliage that provided such perfect shade over those lucky enough to catch a chance to sit under it. Then I noticed something startling to me! The little tree had grown sideways - not up to the sky, but bent to the earth. It was shaped like a sideways **L**. It was a perfectly full grown crooked tree. THIS is why it provided such epic shade. It was like a gorgeous veranda - "*a roofed, open-air gallery*". (Wikipedia) It was the most unique tree I had ever seen - and completely opposite of how every other tree grows, which is generally straight UP. In essence, it was scarred, imperfect, and all kinds of wrongs. Except that it had kept growing. The beautiful tree grew bent with its imperfections, and as it grew its imperfections became its purpose.

That tree spoke to me that day. It was as if it said, "See me? I am you." I remember that in that instance just a simple walk in the park brought tears to my eyes and hope to my soul. That tree was a visual of my life. I thought, wow - I may have grown up sideways and crooked and maybe my soul is not the perfect height of others, but I have a unique purpose no one else does. It is mine BECAUSE of my scars, my imperfections and all kinds of wrongs. *"I am not afraid... I was born to do this." (Joan of Arc)*

My teenage granddaughter researched this topic, with her google search being - 'why do some trees grow sideways?' Here are highlights of what we found, (credits to *https://earthsky.org/author/earthsky/* for great information) and in our own words - tree branches are going to grow towards the light, so whatever way they have to do that is exactly what they will do - even if it means growing SIDEWAYS! The reason is because their leaves NEED the sunlight. Growing crooked may actually protect the leaves from being destroyed by strong winds and other trees cramping their space. (Deep deep deep.) The goal of a tree is to always face the LIGHT even if it has to grow sideways to do that. Really, it's a survival skill that I actually can see in myself now. Wow. Just wow. Mind officially blown. And why I love trees.

I think at this point I just need to own it. Like that tree, just be who I turned out to be. And be okay with it. God doesn't make mistakes, but He can turn broken into whole and imperfect into perfectly imperfect. Maybe imperfect IS the new perfect!

The end of a story is better than its beginning. That tree was in its prime - it was its own crowning glory for all to partake of. I don't think anyone was critical or ashamed of the fact that they were picnicking under a deformed tree. They saw its beauty - they appreciated its purpose, and its crookedness accomplished both. It was beautiful and purposeful only because it was crooked. I couldn't love this more!

Yes, I am like that tree. Abuse twisted my roots and I grew up crooked. As I have matched my foggy memories to actual facts, it has been a slap in the face of my heart. Abuse is not only

sexual. It can be emotional and verbal, without anyone laying a hand on you. I now know I also experienced that too, at a very young age. It totally explains so much to me about myself - my insecurities, my fears, my submissive part to narcissist behavior patterns, and my inability to accept my own worth or to see myself as others do. These are the very things I have struggled with my entire life. I am so over it. I am SO ready to be shade for others under the bent branches of my life. I am SO ready to NOT see myself as flawed anymore. I am SO ready to stop beating myself up for...well, everything, as if the planet's rotation is somehow something I could mess up. The enemy of our soul wants to destroy us. Period. Once we get this, we can see through different eyes.

To me, abuse felt like love in some twisted and warped concept, because in my formative years it was all I knew. THIS is where submissive behavior to abusive patterns comes to play. Abuse is repetitive generally - if you don't stop it, it keeps going - over and over and over, until you get used to it. Thank God I ALSO had pure love to begin to compare it with, and this is where the good things in my life were growing and blossoming alongside. I compare this phenomenon to fragile lily flowers growing up amidst hungry alligators in a Honduran river that I traveled down. There were thousands of them gloriously growing, and fearlessly floating next to glowing evil eyeballs peering from beneath the murky river waters.

My intent is never to trigger others to pain, but more just to expose lies and replace them with truths that abused people can identify with. My hope is always that you will be healed and set free. So briefly I just want to say this - after abuse and if that is all you have known of love you may go searching for more abuse, without realizing it or understanding why. Pure can feel ugly to you, instead of the other way around.

For example, a battered woman who you would think would NEVER get into another violent relationship, will actually be drawn to it. A child who is abused, may grow up to seek solace in the arms of yet another kind of abuser. As I said in earlier chapters, we are drawn to what feels familiar in the depths of our soul, even if it is impure and ugly. THIS is the growing up crooked/bent syndrome (I just made that up). I feel like that is what happened to me.

Abuse bends and twists your roots. Only God can either untwist them (if dealt with early enough into the abuse and WHY we need to scream the FIRST time) or He will use us **in spite of our bentness**. Hallelujah! But God! That's me. That is my book right here. This is the shade I offer - That we can heal. That we can change. That we can see our own value. That we can blossom. That we can be outrageously beautiful. That we can find our purpose and embrace it with relief and JOY.

*"On the mountain heights of Israel I will plant it; it will produce branches and bear fruit and become a splendid cedar. Birds of every kind will nest in it; **they will find shelter in the shade of its branches.**"* (Ezekiel 17:23)

By deciding (or being willing) to take this road less travelled, I found complete exoneration from my past. The freedom and liberation from the spirit of abuse is life changing. I am no longer defined anymore by my roots. Nope. I get to live. I am no longer just surviving - I am thriving! I get to speak LIFE and BLESSING over myself and my family and over the generations from my bloodline. The buck has stopped with me.

"I am no orphan

I'm not a poor man

The Kingdom's now become my own

And with the King I've found a home

He's not just reviving

Not simply restoring

Greater things have yet to come…"

("I Am No Victim" by Kristene DiMarco)

I have finally been able to see myself as beautiful. Not beautiful as in super model kind of beautiful - but beautiful as in the WHO of who God made me. I see my purpose. I even can embrace my imperfections or the things I once called ugly in myself. I realize that my life is meant to be shade for others. My crooked branches are exactly what someone else needs. And I am SO okay with that now.

Perhaps I AM a shade tree which is defined as: *"a tree planted or valued chiefly FOR its shade from sunlight; a tall perennial woody plant having a main trunk and branches forming a distinct elevated crown."* (Wikipedia) Whoa. "...**a distinct elevated crown.**" BAM! THERE it is. My pain (bent and twisted parts) turned to my purpose (to save others) which I now wear as my crowning glory. Wow and wow.

"But blessed is the one who trusts in the LORD, whose confidence is in him. They will be like a tree planted by the water that sends out its roots by the stream. It does not fear when heat comes; its leaves are always green. It has no worries in a year of drought and never fails to bear fruit." (Jeremiah 17:7-8)

Thank you (muchas gracias) little tree in the park of Burbank, California. I saw you that day. I felt you that day. I heard you that day. It turned out to be more than just a walk in the park. Who knew the shade under a simple twisted, bending tree could change a person's life perspective.

CHAPTER NINETEEN
God Uses Broken

~*"The human heart is the only thing whose worth increases the more it is broken "*(Shakieb Orgunwall)~

Have you ever broken a dish? Maybe it was in two pieces, cracked down the middle, and fixable with super glue. Although left with a visible crack, it still worked. Maybe it was a glass dish that you accidentally got too hot (that is all the details you get on THAT) and it literally exploded into hundreds of pieces, all razor sharp and hard to even begin to find them all. Somewhere is a plastic bowl full of broken glass, headed to the broken glass cemetery. To compare our lives to that glass dish and say if we messed up too badly, we then become unusable would be exactly what I am NOT going to say.

"The pages of history

They tell me it's true

That it's never the perfect

It's always the ones with the scars that You use.

It's the rebels and the prodigals.

It's the humble and the weak

All the misfit heroes You chose

Tell me there's hope for sinners like me.

Now I'm just a beggar in the presence of a King

I wish I could bring so much more

But if it's true

You use broken things

Then here I am Lord, I am all Yours."

("Broken Things" by Matthew West)

I want to look at the story of Gideon when God told him to break something – on purpose! Not just break one thing, but 300 of something. Ever hear the story? If YOU have ever been stuck concentrating on your broken parts and anxious over whether or not God could use your life with all its jagged pieces, razor sharp edges and scars, then Gideon's story is for you!

First of all I love the humanness of Gideon; a man God chose to use just as he was. Or who he THOUGHT he was. Gideon was an Israelite harvesting wheat and hiding from his enemies the Midianites. He knew he was a coward, right? He was in hiding. **Except God saw Gideon differently.** (Think on THAT a minute.) He reminds me of the cowardly lion in the movie The Wizard Of Oz. Both had no "couraggggggge". Nevertheless God sent an angel to Gideon to declare him *"a mighty man of valor* (courage)*"* and to tell him he was chosen *"to save Israel from the hand of Midian."* (Judges 6:14)

God sees who we CAN be, in spite of the fact that generally we do NOT see it. God knew Gideon's heart – He knew that there WAS courage there; it was just some hot ashes that needed stirred up to start a fire. There is nothing greater than to see this happen in someone's life – it is like witnessing the light come on! It is that BAM moment! Then, watch out! That person who thought they had no call, no passion, no strength all of a sudden comes to life and is like a lion charging forth.

This is what is stirring in me along my healing journey THAT is because God IS stirred something in me that was already there, albeit way down deep – it was there all along. Speaking of light, here is where you need to see broken things from another angle.

One dark night Gideon and his 300 men marched into the Midianite camp, like a boss! I am thinking this was the moment God was just waiting to pull off! The moment He took a great man in hiding, and made him a mighty man of valor! He instructed Gideon exactly what to do with those 300 men on that dark night, which should have been an easy victory for the unsuspecting Midianites.

300 men with 300 horns and 300 lanterns. That was it. The God of the universe on their side. Oh yes, this was about to go down; it was truly one for the books. THE Book!

First Gideon asked God what to do, then he did it (this is key.) If you ask God for His help or advice or direction, it would be wise to heed what He says – without question. Just do it! Judges 7:20 tells of the plan of attack – *"The three companies blew the trumpets and smashed the jars* (lanterns)..."

Wait. THAT was the plan? Hey Gideon, you will win this war if you all blow your trumpets, scream loudly and break your lighted lanterns. Okay God, whatever you say. YES. Yes, God -WHATEVER YOU SAY! We will recklessly throw abandon to the wind, as we obey Your command. (I wonder what their exact level of fear and excitement was at? Probably off the charts!)

HERE is the most amazing visual you could ever imagine; the visual of a miracle orchestrated by a God who chooses the weakest among us to do the GREATEST things! (Feels sorta/kinda like ME writing books.) When all the lanterns broke, the light would have shined out through every single jagged shard, bounced off each other, became more visible, more multiplied, and more glorious in its presentation! Picture it – hear it! 300 men screaming out, *"A sword for the LORD and for Gideon!"* Coupled with the ear piercing proclamation sound of 300 trumpets, and 300 BROKEN lanterns exploding with violent light in all directions! The Bible says the Midianites fled in TERROR!

I wonder how those 300 men felt; how Gideon himself felt – when the army of the Midianites RAN like little children screaming with fear, into the night. No one died that night. God used 300 regular guys plus the one guy who previously had been cowering in fear hiding under a tree, 300 probably rusty out of tune trumpets, and 300 lanterns that were doomed to be smashed to pieces. An attack had been simulated as if by a larger, fiercer army! Such an amazing visual to represent how God uses the most broken parts of US to shine forth His brightest light. He chooses broken. He uses broken for HIS glory.

Maybe you wonder why I put the story of Gideon in my book and included his story in with my story. Because here I find so much hope. As one who was broken - key word, WAS - I love that all my scars have become my places of beauty, where my story shines the brightest in the dark. I love that God uses broken things. For someone who felt they had been too broken for too long, this story reminds me that it is less about the vessel and more about the God who equips the vessel for usage.

Do you still only see YOUR broken places as useless or unfixable or even unredeemable? God will take broken beyond repair and turn it into a story, or a song, or an invention, or a painting, or a career, or a ministry, or a dance, or a great idea, or a simple blog, or maybe - a book. You will have light pouring out from every broken place, as it is allowed to come forth to heal others. I think what we go through is more about others, than ourselves. God will join you with other broken pieces and your light will grow more powerful – all from broken places. THAT has always been ALL my hope in sharing my story beyond the bolted door in my life.

CHAPTER TWENTY
The Land Before Knowledge

~Innocence was lost because we were NEVER supposed to know about evil. Never~

The very first time I processed any thoughts for the writing of my first book was when I wondered about the significance of the tree of the knowledge of good and evil in the Garden of Eden. It felt to me like we missed something BIG there, in church teachings. So I researched and wrote and thought, and decided that would be the baseline of a book I MIGHT write. It started right there. In fact the title of the book I thought about writing was going to be "The Land Before Knowledge/Return to Innocence" and about how innocence was lost because OF the knowledge of good and evil. We were NEVER supposed to know about evil. Never.

My original first entry for my book looked like this (written March 2020) - *I guess I am just clawing my way back to my own garden, back to find the land (MY land) before knowledge. Let's go back to the original garden – the Garden of Eden, also referred to as Paradise. It was the perfect place to reside, and probably a place all humans are longing to find. I wonder if in some way all of our roots are planted deep in Eden. I wonder if our pull to something else, to something more, to something better is our soul's way of trying to reconnect with what was originally offered to us. We could have all lived in the Garden of Eden. If sin had never crept in, bringing in the knowledge of good and evil, then we would have all had the same home address. However, sin DID creep in and well, the rest is the history of man. Am I understanding maybe that we should never*

EVER have had any knowledge of evil? Sin is something that unfortunately we are ALL born into. It seems we are doomed. It seems there is no way out. It seems evil will win over good. What matters now is that we find our way back to what God always wanted for us, and the reason why He gave us His Son. He wants to return us to the Garden. I have come to believe this IS a real possibility, to find innocence once again within ourselves.

Clearly my heart's cry at the very onset was to find my own innocence lost, and I had really questioned if that was possible.

I find that a lot of what I have learned along my book writing journey has been about trees, so it should be NO surprise that a TREE is where it all began - for ALL of us. *"There were however two important trees in the middle of the garden that were different from the rest. The tree of life and the tree of the knowledge of good and evil. The tree of life as it states gave life, particularly eternal **life**. The other tree would produce **death**."* (Bible Topical Studies)

Adam and Eve were told they could partake of the fruit of any tree in the Garden except the tree of the knowledge of good and evil, because IF they did, their eyes would be opened. It was called forbidden fruit - *"the definition of forbidden fruit is an immoral or illegal pleasure."* (Wikipedia) Immoral. This right here tells me we were NOT meant to know everything. And, we do - to our demise. Research it and find it, in a split second. We currently live IN the time that the Bible calls the increase of knowledge -*"But thou, O Daniel, shut up the words and seal the book, even to the time of the END. Many shall run to and fro, and knowledge shall be increased."* (Daniel 12:4)

I wonder SO much if it was really an apple that was the fall of mankind - or more what that is symbolic of? What did Eve do that cursed us all? What was so good to partake of, that she then dragged down her beloved, perfect specimen of a husband with her? What could possibly have been worth the risk they both took? What was SO tempting? It WAS the knowledge - it was the seduction - it was the danger - and that is the SAME knowledge we all face - that evil thing that Satan uses in the background - in the shadows - in the darkness to ruin our lives. God made all things beautiful - remember, Adam and Eve didn't even know they were naked. This shows their innocence; nothing TO be ashamed of.

There was NO shame in the Garden of Eden. **Until.** Until they partook of the forbidden fruit. *"Then the eyes of both of them were opened, and they knew that they were naked."* (Genesis 3.7). They lost the blessing and the privilege of innocence. Really, think about that and you will see the truth - it is right there in plain view.

Ever wonder why there might be only one bite out of the symbolic apple? (Look around - you can still find it.) Maybe that is all it takes. I mean, it starts with one choice - one thought - one text - one encounter - one drink - one pill - one glance. Sin looks exactly the same for all of us. And Satan only has his same old/same old tricks that he uses.

"The journey from your mind to your hands

Is shorter than you're thinking

Be careful if you think you stand

You just might be sinking

And it's a slow fade

When you give yourself away

It's a slow fade

When black and white have turned to gray

And thoughts invade, choices made

A price will be paid

When you give yourself away."

("Slow Fade" by Casting Crowns)

Wait. I wonder - if the descent downward begins with the infamous one (one glance, one thought…) it's probably the same in reverse, to begin an ASCENT! To change course towards healing,freedom, and redemption is the change of a mind - a choice to do the right thing, a thought, a refusal, a simple NO. Whoa. I have felt so bound by the blurred lines; I have felt the pull to the deadly bug zapper; I have known the slow fade. HOW to reverse THAT is as simple as how it began - a choice, a surrender. This happens (either way) in a split second. I was just thinking of when I was a Girl Scout (yes, I was a Girl Scout once upon a time), and we learned how to make a campfire. We also learned how to put it out which was called starving it. *"Starving a fire: limiting fuel by removing potential fuel from the vicinity of the fire, removing the fire from the mass of combustible materials or by dividing the burning material into smaller fires that can be extinguished more easily."* (Wikipedia) Hmmmm - limiting, removing, dividing, extinguishing, starving. WOW.

All decisions and choices begin with your yes or no. The way to get out of blurred lines and slow fades is one step at a time, in the RIGHT direction. *"Let your Yay be Yay; let your Nay be Nay."* Start the ascent.

The land before knowledge WAS and still IS, innocence! Evil knowledge holds us captive behind a bolted door of secrets and shame, while our soul is crying to be FREE. We must return to Eden in our own hearts. And you CAN. How do I know? Because I DID! I found what I have been missing my entire life.

"You're my hope unbroken.

You're my innocence.

I am free like a river;

I'm a child again."

("Child Again" by NeedToBreathe)

When we open up our heart in its most authentic state (no matter what that is) God shines His light on it NOT to condemn what He sees there, but to redeem and restore us from evil. He takes our worst case possible condition and begins at square ONE to re-do us. Yes, Adam and Eve set the evil knowledge wheels in motion, but God sent Jesus to turn it all around. And, that innocence lost? We CAN find it again in the purity of the love of Jesus, shed abroad in our hearts. The OTHER knowledge on that tree was GOOD, remember.

"Well today I found myself

After searching all these years,

And the man that I saw

Wasn't at all who I thought it'd be.

I was lost when you found me here;

I was broken beyond repair.

Then You came along

And You sang Your song over me.

It feels like I'm born again.

It feels like I'm living

For the very first time

119

For the very first time

In my life."

("Born Again" by Third Day)

I think we could sum up that indeed, first in our hearts and then when we leave this planet - we ARE being wooed BACK to Eden (Heaven). We DO get to go back to the land before knowledge - And NO evil will be there. I can not tell you enough how much my heart swells from this revelation.

CHAPTER TWENTYONE
Recognizing And Discerning Danger

~The power of finding your voice is much like the eruption of a long dormant volcano when it finally explodes from a place so deep that the force affects everything in its path~

My youth leader (from my teenage years) suggested I write a chapter about how to recognize the signs of abuse in someone, because he said how he never saw the signs in me, or didn't realize he WAS looking straight at them. "*The shattering of a heart when being broken is the loudest quiet ever.*" (Carroll Bryant)

In my first book *Beyond The Bolted Door* I talked about how as a teenager I had a double life going, which in turn created two separate personas for me. In fact let me just quote myself -

"As a young teenager is where I clearly remember my mental unraveling because of the continuous sexual exploits, the secrets, the threats, the lies, the manipulation, and the terror that I felt. Terror became a PART of my daily teenage life. I went from being timid and scared of my own shadow to figuring out how to be the life of the party.

If you were the center of attention, you were seen but NOT seen at the same time. I could very aptly appear to be the happiest teenage girl you would ever wish to just please go sit down and be quiet! Funny, but not funny at all. It was an act. It seemed I was living out two parts from an alter ego script. I was able to balance the two roles between my two worlds: with my friends I was a loud, boisterous teen who loved Jesus deeply, but in private I was a fearful, terrorized teen suppressed by the secret of ongoing sexual abuse.

Looking back I realize I did give non subtle cries for help by way of my behavior. It is like the soul inside is screaming for someone – anyone, to pay attention!

For all victims there is a loss of self esteem, social withdrawal or reckless behavior, an avoidance of particular situations or places, and an emotional development that seems delayed or erratic.

All of these signs at some point will be displayed, but if no one seems to take notice, the victim goes underground (so to speak) and a wounded soul will remain wounded, stuck somewhere in the quicksand of time."

Oh the irony of my own behavior - **'See me but don't see me'!** Irony means deliberately contrary to expectation. Bam! And THAT is why we can miss the signs, as many times they are completely hidden from view.

There is a fine line to cross as to whether or not symptoms of abuse are also caused by other stressful situations also - like problems at home/divorce/parent in jail, bullying from other kids at school or anything that brings a child extra anxiety. Therefore I am just going to put a list here of behavior inconsistencies to be on guard for, and to NOT ignore if you see any of them. Apparent changes in sleep, having nightmares, lack of appetite or unusual consumption of food or not eating at all, very distinct mood swings - anger outbursts, excessive fear, too loud or too quiet, maybe suddenly not wanting to be alone or with a particular person, view of body as dirty, unusual sexual terminology, sexual knowledge that is advance for age group. I think for me personally it was my mood swings that were a sign - the out of control loud obnoxious shows of emotion, laughing way too loud all while falling to the floor, OR sobbing my brains out in the corner of a church altar.

In younger kids you could watch for bed wetting, thumb sucking, either being way too shy about their bodies or very much an exhibitionist/ maybe mimicking the behavior of adults in a sexual manner. In teenagers and young adults perhaps self-injury will manifest itself (cutting, pulling out hair, burning skin, injuring animals), drug and alcohol abuse, sexual promiscuity (sexually reckless), depression and anxiety, maybe even suicide attempts. All of these symptoms when compounded into more than one, is a good time to pay attention - ask questions - be like a sniper - alert, on guard and expertly watching from a distance. If you are a parent, grandparent, teacher, babysitter, youth leader or have any sort of responsibility over younger people, PAY ATTENTION. Sometimes it is as simple as we feel like something is 'off'. Maybe it is something you can't put your finger on, so this is where it starts that you keep BOTH eyes open. It may be nothing, but it may be everything. Make friends with your sixth sense.

I think I have a pretty good intuition, and my sixth sense has always seemed a bit sharper than normal, but I really had no idea how to tap into it - and I didn't even identify it as being of importance. I had it - I just didn't access it. A sixth sense is: *"a thing that one knows or considers likely, from instinctive feeling rather than conscious reasoning."* (Wikipedia) In other words, having an awareness that's not capable of being explained in terms of our normal discernment (perception). However, as it has been said - humans are the only creature that even though having such sharp intuition, will nevertheless walk right into danger. There is scientific evidence that indeed our sixth sense COULD save our life, if heeded. I wish I had understood even a small part of this - understood what intuition even was.

Memories that are related to certain circumstances in our life, are uploaded into a sensory part of our brain called the hippocampus - you could call it the brain's 'center stage'. THIS is where our senses are awakened or stimulated to retrieve a memory - thus where the concept of triggers comes from. I feel like all through my life I 'knew' or 'understood' certain things - I could sense them, but without the reasoning or proof, because they were those very secrets I had hidden away. So - I ignored them or shelved them. Looking back, I find this horrifying. Perhaps I could have saved myself - perhaps I could have saved others much sooner. My hope right here right now is to alert you to your own sense of intuition. If someone/something feels wrong, it is probably wrong. If you get an iffy feeling about someone/something, be careful. Step back or step away. Call it a life pause moment. Sixth senses are real and help us discern danger. This can be used in recognizing abuse in others, as well as alerting us TO someone who IS an abuser. Don't fear your sixth sense - exercise it, pay attention to it, strengthen it - see it as an inner alert system.

I read this in an anonymous sexual survivor's story - *"I believe medical professionals should routinely screen for child sexual abuse history, just as they do for allergies, rather than relying on survivors to initiate disclosure."* I couldn't agree more because a child really has NO idea now TO initiate disclosure. Also I think that churches and maybe even schools should make the subject of abuse more open to be discussed, instead of hidden. It doesn't have to be some kind of club you can join or something that puts a target on your back, but if I had known I COULD go talk to someone knowledgeable and trustworthy, maybe I would have. In the late 1960's and early 1970's pretty much nobody anywhere discussed anything deemed shameful. Everyone needs educated about sexual abuse - the ones being abused obviously, but also the ones who need to recognize it happening right before their involuntary blind eyes. Again, knowledge is a weapon.

Those are just some ways to identify someone who may be being abused, but we also need to know how to identify abusers. Red flags or warnings (alerts) for an abuser are sometimes hard to detect - remember that an abuser is already full of secrets so it is a fine art to craft a persona made to deceive. Some of the signs to be aware of are a bad temper, verbal abuse (bullying), very unpredictable and hard to read (an abuser does not WANT to be read), cruelty to animals, very possessive and demanding, manipulation, sabotage, controlling, a blatant disregard other people in general, and forcing themselves sexually is obviously the biggest RED flag.

The abuser was most probably abused. That is NOT an excuse or a free pass - it is just a sad and tragic fact. The pain goes on from generation to generation, until someone stops it. I am hoping to raise an awareness as to the urgency to stop any and all secrets. The only way to change an abuse history, is to be the one who decides "the buck stops with me." Victims either stay victims, beaten down and buried under the weight of shame OR in worst case scenarios they too become abusive.

Abuse never lets you have the power of a choice. You are not given the option to say no. Abuse never lets YOU decide. It just takes. It just demands. It just manipulates. It gives you no options. The abuser is deftly able to make you believe that indeed you DID choose. Maybe in their delusional mind your silence and submission is a loud, resounding yes, as if you chose when you did not refuse. So you begin to question WHY were you abused? Was I an easy target? Was I deserving of it? Did I provoke it? Did I just fall for it? Was my silence a signal of acceptance? Yuk. Just yuk. To think an innocent child or an emotionally immature teen or a battered woman would choose to be abused. An abuser overpowers you, and makes you feel powerLESS. They run on the fuel of fear induced power.

Having said that, the power of finding your voice is much like the eruption of a long dormant volcano when it finally explodes from a place so deep that the force affects everything in its path. The lava IS your voice. Remember that visual as you decide to take back your choice and your power.

"Open up ancient gates. Open up ancient doors, and let the King of glory enter." (Psalm 24:9) You have heard the term "ancient history", as it speaks of days and times gone by. Ancient means: *"belonging to the very distant past and no longer in existence."* (Wikipedia) So, in referring to our bolted doors, we are to open them and let Jesus enter. Whoa. That is so deep.

We fear what lies behind those doors - all the secrets of our buried pasts, and yet we are to OPEN those doors NOT so what's there will kill us, but so that JESUS can enter and take over. As we open our ancient bolted door though corroded shut and a visual of destruction, hope is not abandoned as the glory of JESUS now shines forth healing the past, the present, and the future. Curses will be broken and blessings will be restored for generations to come.

"I'm slowly learning to be grateful

Found some purpose in all the hurt

Now I'm rediscovering what I'm worth

Just takes one step to turn the tables

But I had to take it first

Now I'm healing

Now I'm healing

I'm here unashamed

I found strength through the pain

What was broken is standing again."

("Healing" by Riley Clemmons)

"The things you do for yourself are gone when you are gone, but the things you do for others remain as your legacy." (Kalu Ndukwe Kalu) Each one of us has a chance and a choice TO change history. Another quote from USA gymnast Jessica Howard, *"All we need is ONE person to do the right thing!"* We must decimate and destroy shame, silence, and secrets for the sake of generations to come.

"I call heaven and earth to record this day against you, that I have set before you life and death, blessing and cursing: therefore choose life, that both thou and thy seed may live." (Deuteronomy 30:19)

CHAPTER TWENTYTWO
He Knows MY Name

~In her utter brokenness and despair, she recognized Jesus simply by hearing Him call her name~

Who was Mary Magdalene? She was one of Jesus' disciples. More than just being one of them, she was the FIRST one and the ONLY woman. She was present at the landmark days in Jesus' story – His crucifixion and then His resurrection. "*When Jesus rose early on the first day of the week, he appeared first to Mary Magdalene,*" (Mark 16:9) Surely she must have been the cream of the crop, lady in waiting, precious jewel polished and shined to have received such a calling upon her life.

Oh, wait – the rest of Mark 16:9 says, "*…out of whom He had driven seven demons.*" This is the one Jesus chose to be His first follower. I don't know about you, but I LOVE everything about this!

Well, if there ever was a more tortured soul than she, I do not know! She was demon-possessed, and not with just one demon but with SEVEN demons. Seven being the number of 'completion' it would seem that to have seven demons was completely too much of too much despair in her life – an overload of evil torment. She must have cried. How she must have screamed. She must have loathed her life. How downcast she must have felt. An outcast. The subject of gossipers. Definitely, the avoided one. The shamed one. A prisoner in her own internal hell. Day after day after day.

Until. Until she heard Jesus call her name. *"Jesus said to her, "Mary!"* (John 20:16) Her immediate response was, she turned to face Him. I wonder if her first thought was what I myself would have been thinking - HE KNOWS MY NAME!

And yes I know He delivered her from her 7 demons. I am sure He addressed them to leave her with His powerful authority over them. But I LOVE that the very first thing He said was HER name.

I absolutely know that Jesus wasn't the least bit threatened by those seven demons. He was only interested in saving her soul. He saw past the demons in her, and He saw HER. And He KNEW her. He valued her. As a result, she knew it was her creator. Whoa. Shrouded in the darkness of her utter brokenness and despair, she recognized Jesus simply by hearing Him call her name.

THEN He took care of her demons – after she responded to His call. Stop right here. For me personally, this is everything. Jesus saw her as is. Not just full of sin, but full of demons. Not just full of failures, but full of demons. This seems to be the worst of the worst condition for a human to end up in. YET Jesus went to where she was. He searched for her. He didn't come with religion or magic or rituals or formulas.

HELLO! He simply called her by her name. *"Mary!"*

Oh to hear Him call her name. It wrecked her and saved her and transformed her in a word, and that ONE word was her name. Does anyone else find this mind-blowing? First of all, ALL the love of eternity was in that voice. Second of all, All the hope. All the deliverance. And all the destiny. It was her moment to turn and face her creator, and to know her place in His creation.

She was there at His crucifixion – *"Now there stood by the cross of Jesus his mother, and his mother's sister, Mary the wife of Cleophas, and Mary Magdalene."* (John 19:25) She was there at His resurrection – *"The first day of the week cometh Mary Magdalene early, when it was yet dark, unto the sepulcher, and seeth the stone taken away from the sepulcher."* (John 20:1)

"Before I formed you in the womb I knew you; before you were born I set you apart..." (Jeremiah 1:5) The same God who created us, knows us by our name IN our mother's womb. He had set YOU apart before you were even born. *"...The Lord called me from the womb, from the body of my mother He named my name."* (Isaiah 49:1)

Can YOU hear Him calling to you? I did. Jesus said to me, "Corine!" I turned to face Him. And it has forever changed me.

CHAPTER TWENTYTHREE
Who Jesus Is To Me

~Jesus is the one who carries me, the one who fights for me, and the one who looks out for me. I hold nothing back. No more clenched fists. No more fear~

"Do you feel that empty feeling?

'Cause shame's done all its stealin'

And you're desperate for some healin'

Let me tell you 'bout my Jesus."

("My Jesus" by Anne Wilson)

Looking back, I would have to describe my relationship with Jesus as reserved/not on His part, but definitely on mine! I had faith and convictions instilled in me by my sister (before my adoption) and then by my adoptive mother (after adoption). I have been blessed with quite a few women in my life who instilled IN me my unshakeable faith. I laugh nervously as I say that He knew I needed MANY mothers. What I did not have was a working, loving relationship with a father figure. And THIS is where my reservedness plays into my relationship with Jesus. I think one of the most important pieces of my life puzzle that I needed to find was who I was TO Him AS a father. Not what others have told me, taught me or even what just feels right. No. And not even how I saw myself, since indeed my self image was badly flawed from sexual abuse.

"I cover up the pain that I'm lost in

'Cause I wanna be enough and it's exhausting.

Trying so hard but really I'm just wearing my heart out

And I find myself right on the verge of a breakdown.

Then You hold me in Your hands,

Remind me who You are and who I am.

I was born broken so You can make me whole

I'll bring my dirt and let You wash over me like water.

I was born to need You, to wipe the tears I cry.

Yes, You made me a child so You could be my Father.

I'm Your child and You're my Father.

Even when I'm lost and I don't feel found;

You lead me, protect me, bring me home.

I'm weak and afraid but You never let go.

And I don't have to hide 'cause You already know,

Already know You're still my Father"

("Father" by Jeremy Camp)

That song? Those lyrics? Years and years ago I would have NEVER been able to listen to it. 100% nope! The reservedness I spoke of was born of abuse. When your perception of love is tarnished, you don't gravitate to pure love - you move away from it, and though maybe not totally, you do hold back with invisible fists clenched in your soul. I now have a real relationship where

I finally get to be the child and I finally get to know and trust the one I call Father. I finally see me how Jesus sees me.

Jesus Christ has SO many names that describe His character - King of Kings, Lamb of God, The Good Shepherd, Bread of Life, Lord of Glory, Savior, Redeemer, Morning Star (my favorite because it speaks of signaling the dawn of a NEW day), Great High Priest, Chief Cornerstone, Messiah, Light of the World, Teacher, The Way/The Truth/The Life. All of those names - yes, I could relate to each of them. All those years I loved Jesus, believed in Him, and followed Him, but because of the portion I had held back, I didn't know Him fully and completely. However, He knew ME fully and completely. Let me tell you who He was TO me personally during those years - He protected me. He was my safe place. He was the only one who saw my tears in the night. He held me in the darkest parts of those nights when I felt so small and so alone. He miraculously strengthened me to face every day with optimism and hope, regardless of the long night before. He put people in my life who cultivated the best parts of me. He never was mean or overbearing with me. God is NOT a narcissist - His love is pure and unconditional/agape love. Let's define that word agape - *"Greek agapē, in the New Testament, the fatherly love of God for humans."* (Wikipedia) Ah, there it is - father, the part of Him I rejected. I feel like all the other true representations of Him I was accepting of - my protector, counselor, provider, friend, comforter, teacher, the faithful One - faithful to ME. But my father? Nope. Too personal - too close - too intimate.

I said all that to say THIS - ah, but who Jesus is to me NOW? Now Jesus is my Father figure - the one who carries me, the one who fights for me, and the one who looks out for me. I hold nothing back. No more clenched fists. No more fear. *"Then I said to you, 'Do not be terrified; do not be afraid of them. The LORD your God, who is going before you, **will fight for you**, as He did for you in Egypt, before your very eyes, and in the wilderness. There you saw how the LORD **your God carried you, as a father carries his son (or daughter) all the way you went until you reached this place**."* (Deuteronomy 1:29-31)

A father advocates for his children. At this season of my life in my healing journey, I see that I was ready for an advocate/a champion, ready for a father. Accepting Him AS my father, I get to experience what that is supposed to feel like. Mostly for me, it feels safe. I feel relief. When you feel safe, you are not looking over your shoulder - you are not suspicious - you are not looking for a devil around every corner - you can breathe - you can rest - you can trust - all fear is gone. And I DO mean ALL fear. You know why? *"There is no fear in love; but perfect love casts out fear, because fear involves torment. But he who fears has not been made perfect in love."* (1 John 4:18) Fear involves torment - and there it is - torment is harsh/grievous physical or mental suffering. Jesus is the opposite of that. And why I can now wholeheartedly accept Him as my Father. And finally, I know Him fully and completely.

"I will tremble at no other name.

My heart's surrendered to no other reign.

I will bow at no other throne,

And rest my heart at no other home.

You take my breath with every starry night;

Show Your power in downtown city light.

You are taller than the highest of the hills,

And stronger than the walls we try to build.

You blind me with the beauty of Your face

And draw me close with Your divine embrace.

Speak to me with healing in Your words

And fix the things I didn't know were hurt.

You invented all of time and space

Called the morning and midnight into place;

Made the mountains and tamed the wildest seas,

And still You set Your holy eyes on me."

("Tremble" by Lauren Daigle)

CHAPTER TWENTYFOUR
Hope Returns

~The key is to keep moving forward - against all odds, in spite of the pain, no matter how hard it is - and the day WILL come when you feel like you can exhale your breath again~

Hope returns. Two words where I live in the space in between. The definition of hope: "*to cherish a desire with anticipation, to want something to happen or be true.*" (Merriam/Webster) Before hope can return, there is work to do. Hope ironically keeps you going TO see itself fulfilled. You need hope to believe IN hope. So, why does hope need to return? Return is an act of coming back. That means it was lost somewhere along the way.

"So this is how it feels when standing strong

Turns into barely even holding on

The plans you had are shattered on the floor

And your fear tells your faith,

There's no use in praying those prayers anymore

When your world is crashing, when your knees hit the ground

When your heart is asking, "What do I do now?"

Just when you think it can't get worse

Hold on, that's when hope returns."

("Hope Returns" by Matthew West)

I had not planned to talk about grief in this book, because I guess I had reserved the task of grief only to the death of a person. However, grief is defined by many words - sadness, anguish, pain, distress, torment, affliction, agony, sorrow, suffering and loss of HOPE. (Ah, THERE it is.) I really never thought of it as being all of those things, but yes - indeed it is. And we don't only grieve for those who have died.

I am currently grieving for myself and the parts of my life I lost as well as the parts I never had to begin with. Grief is emotional suffering, not just limited to death but to ANY loss and ALL regret. When someone is overwhelmed by their grief we refer to them as 'grief stricken'. It is very deep and intense, and can be a debilitating thing. Were you ever taught about it? I was not. Maybe it is because it's on a 'need to know' basis - you don't need to know, until you need to know!

So, IF you need to know, here you go - let's talk about grieving for the parts of us we lost because of any kind of abuse.

I remember one night many years ago when my husband Jack and I were fast asleep - our bed was near the window, and all of a sudden we heard our van drive away! I remember that exact feeling of violation - someone stole our van right out from under us and there was nothing we could do about it (at the moment). When it WAS located days later, it was down over a hill - tires missing, everything that was useful was stripped out of it and it was just the shell of the treasured family van we had known and loved. I never forgot that feeling, as if evil had touched us. It is a violation to your innocence/virtue/goodness to have someone steal something that was yours, or should have been yours. THIS is how I feel now as I walk through the agony of realizing all the parts of me I never get to see again. I finally see that I am grief stricken, and just understanding THAT is half the battle. I am at that 'need to know' point. And maybe YOU need to know too.

In grieving there are many stages you can go through, and not in any order but good to recognize them when they show up. Anger. Denial. Shock. Regret. Depression. What ifs. Soul crushing sadness. *"The ax forgets, but the tree remembers."* (African proverb) The final stage is most likely 'acceptance' (agreeing to receive something) and the one that is the hardest but the most valuable. With the acceptance, comes the return of HOPE. This particular part of the healing journey begins with grief but ends with hope. Isaiah 38:17 declares: *"Behold, it was for my welfare that I had great bitterness; and in love You have delivered my life from the pit of destruction."* It does NOT seem to make sense, except that is exactly how it works.

> *"There's hope for the hopeless*
>
> *And all those who've strayed*
>
> *Come sit at the table*
>
> *Come taste the grace*
>
> *There's rest for the weary*
>
> *Rest that endures*
>
> *Earth has no sorrow*
>
> *That heaven can't cure."*

("Come As You Are" by David Crowder)

I love that one line - *"Earth has NO sorrow that heaven can't cure."* I 100% believe that to be true. All my sorrows - all my pain - all my regrets - all my what ifs - as I lay each of them down at the feet of Jesus, they are cured (healed/restored), and

I trade them all for - HOPE. *"Hope is being able to see that there is light despite all of the darkness."* (Desmond Tutu)

Maybe holding my secret seemed less painful than trading it in, or just letting it go. I mean, really - who wants to invite pain to the table? What I am working at understanding now is that this pain of healing I am in, is a much better place to BE. There is something terribly exhausting to the pit of your soul to carry around something hidden that no one knows about, therefore no one can help you carry it OR help you get rid of it. I would like to interject here that if YOU have held back sharing a painful part of your life for fear of the repercussions (whatever that might look like to you), you need to know that YES letting it go will be weighty and difficult, but NOT as heavy and grueling as the burden you have had in carrying it in secret.

Hope IS returning for me and the key word is IS. While I am writing this book about healing from my healing, I AM healing. Sounds so ridiculously simple but has been anything BUT simple. Hear me on this one - healing is a process. Encountering one pain at a time and working through it. One step at a time. Let yourself feel and experience the pain coupled with the freedom. It means you are coming back to life! Hold on, because you ARE experiencing HOPE returning. Keep going. Just like one day my new knees all of a sudden one day seemed to bend easiest, with less pain? That is how it feels in my soul.

"There is a time for everything,

and a season for every activity under the heavens:

a time to be born and a time to die,

a time to plant and a time to uproot

*a time to kill and **a time to heal**,*

a time to tear down and a time to build,

a time to weep and a time to laugh"

(Ecclesiastes 3)

Just like our natural seasons change, the seasons of our lives change. And that is needful and necessary. The key is to keep moving forward - against all odds, in spite of the pain, no matter how hard it is - and the day WILL come when you feel like you can exhale your breath again, because healing has finished its work in you.

"Someday you're gonna look back on this moment of your life as such a sweet time of grieving. You'll see that you were in mourning, and your heart was broken, but your life was changing." (Elizabeth Gilbert) I wept when I read that quote - I would have NEVER expected that to be true, but for me it has been! All I have grieved. all I have lost, all I have mourned, my heart that was broken - all of it has changed me for the better.

EPILOGUE

Through the past few years in my soul I have harbored a running list of my regrets, failures, consequences and all things I deem myself somehow responsible for. I seemed to be constantly rehearsing it. So over and over and over I would cry; I would worry; I would have anxiety; I would feel worthless; I would lose sleep; and then finally just feel useless and hopeless - because I WANTED to fix it ALL. While I was trying to heal, I thought healing meant FIXING. I totally get overwhelmed with all of that because I can NOT fix the past or its repercussions - it is impossible. Today I heard God softly say, "No, NOT fix. Heal."

And I knew instantly what that meant - I am not able to FIX the past; I just need to HEAL from it. GOD miraculously is the one who redeems lost time. HE is the one who mends a broken heart. HE is the one who sets a captive free. I can NOT fix what is unfixable. But He is not even asking me to. He just wants ME to heal. If I heal, then THAT is the legacy I can leave behind.

Heal. Just heal. Whatever that looks like for you, maybe you already know. Maybe you have been questioning the process, or wondering what it even looks like. Healing comes with surrender, admission, truth, forgiveness, acceptance, and a whole laundry list of painful things that hurt before they make us better. BUT when you have healed, then you can change the future, and there lies freedom for the generations to come.

We MUST find healing. We don't need to be fixed, or TO fix - we just need to heal. "By HIS wounds, YOU have been healed." (1 Peter 2:24) Find the peace of closure that is in these words. Be healed.

Does my healing mean I am now perfect and I never will have another struggle, or another trigger, or another sharp pain reminding me from whence I came? No. What it DOES mean is what I will end my book with - it feels like going home. That feeling when all is right with the world. Peace. Relief. Joy. Contentment. *"My mission in life is not merely to survive, but to thrive; and to do so with some passion, some compassion, some humor, and some style."* (Maya Angelou)

My bolted door has been opened. Beyond it I have traveled my own road less traveled, and now it is full of my footprints. I have kicked up the gravel and scattered the leaves. My faith has matured. It is well with my soul. The healing from the healing has done its work., and I bid it farewell.

ACKNOWLEDGEMENTS

I would like to recognize those who walked with me on different footpaths of my recent less traveled road. *"If I have seen further, it is by standing on the shoulders of giants."* (Isaac Newton)

First to my son Joseph Channell/JackMorgan Productions, who is my rockstar book cover designer and editor in chief. I give him all my fragments of ideas from the brain of a writer NOT an artist, and he then creates a visual masterpiece! He also answers my endless technical questions, and gives me invaluable professional help and input for which I am most grateful.

Katie Cobb - my number one reviewer of every word in my book. As I proceeded in my writing journey, I knew that I could send her a chapter or a sentence or a one word change for her critique or opinion, and she would faithfully and quickly respond. Really, she has been like having my own personal cheerleader! I value her encouragement, thoughts and opinions, which come from a heart of love and empathy.

To my prayer warrior Eleanore Hurst who calls down heaven in her prayer closet on my behalf, because really - what could I hope to accomplish without the backing of heaven? I have no accurate words for how needful her prayers have been. They have been life giving, and have bore me on angel wings when I simply would have fallen straight out of the sky.

My grandchildren who intentionally and unintentionally give me remarkable insights, and they cheer me on from the sidelines with their faith IN me and unconditional love FOR me - "I love you (each) to the moon and back."

Also, I want to shout out those who have so often filled in the blank spaces and inspired me in between the lines of this book - Dawn Price, Shaunna Griffith, Daisy Channell, Abigail Clement, Deborah Mooney, Michelle Felder and Kate Burkhard. I have valued all your input, advice, prayers, and healing words of love to 'take as prescribed'.

And a special THANK YOU to those who volunteered to pre-read my book in its raw/unedited/every evolving form, as well as provide a written book review for within the book itself. This process matters SO much to me, because this is where I learn if my writing accomplished the purpose I was aiming for. Much like, you would make sure of the success of your original cookie recipe before adding it to a community cookbook. The recipe MUST be tried and true. So, special thanks to Milinda Mugford, Carissa Cron, Luke Worle, Mary Roth, Katie Cobb, Joe Wooley and Katrina Clement.

Without ALL of your time and love to cheer me on, I might have crashed somewhere along the road and there remained.

TRIBUTE

05/05/ 1958-02/19/2022 Vickie Morgan-Hudson

On this final weekend of my book editing, I experienced the loss of a dear lifelong friend Vickie Morgan-Hudson. She called me C and I called her V. Through the years she has been a source of pure infectious laughter, and prophetic God words spoken into my life. I was thinking how I would miss that laugh and those words. I then remembered something she had left me in my messages, so I went and retrieved it. Timing is everything. So I want to pay tribute to her, for her unwavering belief in me and for having a vital part in my writing journey of BOTH books.

A year ago right before my first book came out, she messaged me this:

"C, it's me V! I thought about you yesterday and your book when I was reading a passage in Isaiah which talked about Hepzibah being no longer forsaken. *"You shall no more be termed Forsaken, and your land shall no more be termed Desolate; you shall be called My Delight."* It's found in Isaiah 62: 4. Hephzibah means not only someone who evokes delight, but also *"one who is guarded; a protected one."* That's you, C."

Thank you V, for cheering me on for the past 42 years.

A few days before she died, I wrote this in her honor - Why we should all keep going, fulfill our own purpose and never give up, is because none of our stories are finished, until ALL of our stories are finished.

APPENDIX

"Stories wait for endings, but SONGS are brave things bold enough to sing when all they know is darkness. "

("To Write Love on Her Arms" by Jamie Tworkowski)

I have quoted a few lines from each of these referenced songs below, and I would recommend you search and listen to each song in its fullness, as they are each soothing healing balm for the weary soul. As I penned my own thoughts, listening to each of these songs activated deep, inward feelings in my soul. In the words of my son, *Songs are nostalgic. It's not just emotion; it's visceral. You can taste and feel it."*

"Child Again" by NeedToBreathe
"Hold On To Me" by Lauren Daigle
"Rise Up" by Andra Day
"I Am No Victim" by Kristine DiMarco
"Different" by Micah Tyler
"Fear Is A Liar" by Zach Williams
"You Say" by Lauren Daigle
"Scars" by I Am They
"In Jesus Name(God Of Possible)" by Katy Nichole
"I Will Fear No More" by The Afters
"You Can't Lose Me" by Faith Hill
"Slow Fade" by Casting Crowns
"The Unraveling" by Cory Ashbury
"He Makes All Things New" by Big Daddy Weave
"I'm Ready Now" by Plumb
"Don't You" by Jordan Smith
"Born Again" by Third Day

"If We're Honest" by Francesca Battistelli
"Undone" by Kim Walker Smith
"Broken Things" by Matthew West
"Father" by Jeremy Camp
"My Jesus" by Anne Wilson
"Tremble" by Lauren Daigle
"Hope Returns" by Matthew West
"Come As You Are" by David Crowder
"Healing" by Riley Clemmons